MW01200554

THE
STEWARD
PLAN

THE
STEWARD
PLAN

Understanding God's Design for Your Finances

John A. Madison, CPA

ELM HILL

A Division of
HarperCollins Christian Publishing

www.elmhillbooks.com

© 2019 John A. Madison, CPA

The STEWARD Plan

Understanding God's Design for Your Finances

All rights reserved. No portion of this book may be reproduced, stored in a retrieval system, or transmitted in any form or by any means—electronic, mechanical, photocopy, recording, scanning, or other—except for brief quotations in critical reviews or articles, without the prior written permission of the publisher.

Published in Nashville, Tennessee, by Elm Hill, an imprint of Thomas Nelson. Elm Hill and Thomas Nelson are registered trademarks of HarperCollins Christian Publishing, Inc.

Elm Hill titles may be purchased in bulk for educational, business, fund-raising, or sales promotional use. For information, please e-mail SpecialMarkets@ ThomasNelson.com.

All Scripture quotations, unless otherwise indicated, are taken from the Holy Bible, New International Version®, NIV®. Copyright © 1973, 1978, 1984, 2011 by Biblica, Inc.® Used by permission of Zondervan. All rights reserved worldwide. www.Zondervan.com. The "NIV" and "New International Version" are trademarks registered in the United States Patent and Trademark Office by Biblica, Inc.®

Scripture quotations marked CEV are from the Contemporary English Version. Copyright © 1991, 1992, 1995 by American Bible Society. Used by permission.

Scripture quotations marked ESV are from the ESV® Bible (The Holy Bible, English Standard Version®). Copyright © 2001 by Crossway, a publishing ministry of Good News Publishers. Used by permission. All rights reserved.

Scripture quotations marked KJV are from the King James Version. Public domain.

Scripture quotations marked NKJV are from the New King James Version®. © 1982 by Thomas Nelson. Used by permission. All rights reserved.

Scripture quotations marked NLT are from the Holy Bible, New Living Translation. © 1996, 2004, 2007, 2013, 2015 by Tyndale House Foundation. Used by permission of Tyndale House Publishers, Inc., Carol Stream, Illinois 60188. All rights reserved.

Cover Design by K.Winters.

Library of Congress Cataloging-in-Publication Data

Library of Congress Control Number: 2019912107

ISBN 978-1-400328079 (Paperback)
ISBN 978-1-400328086 (eBook)

To everyone
desiring to be the financial steward
God has called them to be

About John Madison and Dayspring Financial Ministry

John Madison is a Certified Public Accountant (CPA) with over thirty years of experience striving to assist his clients in meeting their financial and business goals. In addition to completing a bachelor of science degree in accounting, he also holds a master of science degree in personal financial planning. He retired from full-time work as a CPA at the age of 49 and now pursues his calling to teach biblically-based stewardship principles through Dayspring Financial Ministry. In addition to providing individualized financial counseling, John also presents live workshops on Biblical stewardship, as well as how to maximize the tax benefits from tithes and offerings.

For more information, please visit: www.dayspringfm.com

ENDORSEMENTS FROM JOHN'S HOME CHURCH
Winn's Baptist Church
Glen Allen, Virginia

"John and his family have served faithfully in our church for over 15 years. He has felt increasingly led to teach on the same subject as his vocational expertise: finances. Our congregation, and I personally, have benefitted so much as John explains biblical principles for handling money!"

PASTOR JEFF BRAUER
SENIOR PASTOR

"The Steward Plan is a roadmap for your personal finances and is completely based on principles in Scripture. John's work is one of the most interesting, comprehensive, and yet concisely written books you will read on personal finance and it will quite possibly change your life. It explains all you need to know about personal finance from a Biblical perspective."

PASTOR DOUG ARNOLD
ASSOCIATE PASTOR

ACKNOWLEDGEMENTS

I t's often been said that unexpected surprises are a "God thing". He is constantly at work all around us, moving in our lives to bring good to us and to others. I consider this book to be one of those "God things." It was never in my plans to write a book, but looking back now I see how He was at work the entire time, arranging seemingly unrelated events, that culminated in the publishing of *The Steward Plan*. So, I'd like to thank Him for giving me this opportunity to potentially help more people with financial stewardship education than I ever imagined that I could. Truly a "God thing".

Additionally, I'd like to thank my wife, Rachel, for her steadfast devotion, encouragement and support. Our journey together has been a long and winding road, with both peaks and valleys, as I suppose most relationships experience. Through it all, I know there is no one I'd rather travel through life with more than with her. Thanks, Rae. I love you.

Finally, thank you to the many others who invested their time and wisdom training, encouraging, challenging and when needed, admonishing me. *The Steward Plan* and Dayspring Financial Ministry wouldn't exist without the seeds you planted over the years.

Important Disclosure

Personal finance is most importantly "personal." Each reader will be in a different situation regarding their age, debt, income, investments, health, etc. Therefore, it is not possible to write a book about personal finance that would provide one set of recommendations that is appropriate for every situation. Accordingly, please keep the following disclosure in mind as you read:

The recommendations provided in this book are educational in nature and not intended to be specific recommendations for any particular individual. The goal is to educate and inform the reader of available options, with the ultimate decision being theirs. Please consult the appropriate tax, investment, insurance, or financial planning expert before making any final decisions.

Fortunately, the Bible is the Word of God—perfect, complete, and infallible. On it, we can place our trust. Focus first on the principles taught in God's Word, then consider the application of the principle to your exact situation. I hope, of course, that the recommendations provided in this book will help guide you to the course of action God would have for you.

Dayspring Financial Ministry provides personal financial counseling to those needing assistance, or desiring an independent opinion, about the proper financial decision for their family. Contact us to discuss whether Dayspring can help you in your stewardship journey.

John A. Madison, CPA, CRPC, AWMA
www.dayspringfm.com / john@dayspringfm.com

TABLE OF CONTENTS

Introduction and Testimony

B ible scholars have determined that there are over 2,000 verses in the Bible that concern money. Surprisingly, this is more than the references for love, faith, grace, and heaven. God understood that His greatest creation would often place wealth above the Creator Himself. These verses serve to not only warn us of many common money dangers, but also to teach us a better way. His way to manage His wealth. And make no mistake—it is His wealth. No matter the level of financial success we may experience during our time on earth, we will not enter eternity with even the smallest shred of it. When we stand before a God who created the universe and all that is in it, I'm quite sure He won't be impressed by the wealth we accumulated, but He will be interested in what we did with it, whether much or little.

A steward is defined as one who manages another's property, finances, or other affairs. No term better captures the role we are supposed to play concerning God's wealth. We are the steward—the caretaker and manager—not the owner. Nowhere in the Scripture does God ever transfer ownership to us. Still, many incorrectly claim ownership of their possessions and manage them as they see fit in pursuit of their goals. I'm guilty of such behavior prior to my salvation, and unfortunately, I battle it even today as my flesh will still attempt to lead me astray, even after over twenty years saved by His grace.

While this book is not about me, it seems proper to briefly share my personal and financial testimony with you, the reader. I certainly have not approached this process with perfection in my past; quite the opposite, actually.

I was raised in church and responded to the invitation when I was around seven or eight years old. In retrospect, I understand now that I went forward because that was what I thought I was supposed to do. There was no ill intent or deception involved. I simply didn't understand what salvation truly meant.

With no spiritual grounding, it came as no surprise that my college years led me away from any semblance of a relationship with God. Suddenly, fitting in with my new "friends" took on increased importance. I started drinking alcohol in college, rarely at first, but gradually more over time. Academically, after a rough freshman year due to my apathy, I began to do well in school despite the mess that I made of my personal life. I was married early in my junior year and, not surprisingly, was ill-prepared for the responsibilities of my new role. In my arrogance, I foolishly thought I had my life under control and there was no room or need for God in my life.

I graduated early with my bachelor's degree in accounting, having already passed the difficult Certified Public Accounting exam on my first attempt during my senior year of college. Hired by one of the largest international accounting firms, I considered myself to be a success, which I was in the eyes of the world. While fortunate to graduate college with no student loan debt, I quickly remedied that status by immediately purchasing a new convertible even though I had no money. Soon, I bought a house. With a house purchase comes the new furniture and appliances. Everything was, of course, bought with credit.

It didn't take long for the financial house of cards to collapse. Money woes contributed to a difficult marital situation, leading to a separation and divorce soon after our son was born. While I was advancing in my professional life, I found myself living in a cheap apartment, deeply in debt. I left the marriage with minimal property, but I took on the responsibility to repay most of the loans we accumulated during our marriage. For a year and a half, I ate my meals sitting on the floor because I didn't have a table and chairs. I had a thirteen-inch television sitting on a milk crate and copy paper boxes to hold my clothes. Every penny counted and the stress of worrying about having enough money to pay my bills was relentless and unending. I did, though, always have enough money to buy alcohol and my drinking continued, I suppose, as a coping mechanism to deal with the stress of the situation. I still had no use for God.

Over time, I was able to slowly pay down and then eliminate the debts. I promised myself then that I would never allow myself to get into that sort of predicament again. I was blessed to meet my wife, Rachel, during this time and our relationship blossomed into marriage soon thereafter.

Through our first few years of marriage, my career continued to advance. I was better—but far from perfect—with money too. To the world, it would seem that I had it all: a nice home, beautiful wife with whom I had two daughters, two new cars in the driveway. I even had the picket fence in the backyard! I was, though, utterly empty and miserable.

In Genesis, the Scripture tells us that God spoke everything into existence except for His greatest creation—man. He molded Adam out of mud with His hands and breathed life into him. A much more intimate and personal creation versus simply speaking him into existence. I believe that He created us with a need for Him, a hole in our hearts, if you will, that only He can fill. In my attempts to fill this hole on my own, I doubled down on alcohol, drinking every night, sometimes to extreme excess. I knew something had to change, but I didn't know what to change or how to do it.

In the midst of this downward spiral, I had the opportunity when visiting my parents to attend their church in Woodstock, Georgia. I'll admit that I didn't want to go, but when your mom asks a favor, you do it. I still recall that Saturday night telling Rachel how much I needed a drink, as I refrained from alcohol for a few days while staying with my nondrinking parents.

The next morning, I went to church, content to sit through the service and then get to lunch before the crowds arrived. God had other plans. As the sermon progressed, I felt an overwhelming conviction about how I was conducting my life. While I heard no audible sound, God's voice was clear in my head and in my heart. He told me that He was what I was looking for and the only solution to the problems in my life. Internally,

I was stunned. When we stood to sing the invitation hymn, I couldn't make a sound. The lump in my throat and the tears in my eyes prevented it. I couldn't explain what was going on and stood there in silence. Even more amazing, when I left the service, my desire to drink was gone. Completely, 100% gone. I had absolutely no desire to drink even though I was complaining about it the very night before.

I listened to more sermons on the drive back to Virginia and the first thing I did when we arrived home was to pour every beer I had down the kitchen drain. The mere smell of it turned my stomach. God had worked a miracle in me. It took me until the next Sunday, August 30, 1998, to wrap my head around what happened and ask God to forgive me and come into my life. Now, nearly twenty-one years since that day, I have never once had the desire to drink alcohol again.

Professionally, my career continued to move forward with more vigor as my mind was clear from alcohol. On January 1, 2000, I started my freelance accounting company, which God blessed tremendously over the years. I continued to make some mistakes with money. I invested based on what did well the previous year. I bought the wrong types of life insurance. We didn't budget our money. But we did stay out of debt, and as each mistake manifested itself, I learned the right way to handle that issue—God's way. Our wealth grew rapidly during these years as God blessed us and we became better stewards of His resources.

I learned as well that I enjoyed teaching, having taught our Sunday school class for seven years. Through a series of work-related events, I had the opportunity to move my freelance accounting work to part-time status. God had graciously provided the resources necessary to support our expenses outside of my work income. Combining my desire to teach with my interest in personal finance, I tried my hand at blogging and coaching as a second business. I knew the fear and anxiety caused by money problems, as well as the relief that can come from stewarding God's resources His way, and I wanted to help others through the same journey I walked.

While I was able—I hope—to help a few coaching clients, I never felt at peace with the business-like approach I took to my encore career.

Honestly, I floundered for some time with it, not sure what to do. Do I shut down completely? Should I change something about it? And if so, what?

After much prayer, God began to share with me a different approach. Rachel and I often wondered why God had blessed us financially as He had. It became clearer to me that He had done so in order for me to approach financial counseling as a ministry to help others, not as a new profit center. Eventually, this conviction led me to create **Dayspring Financial Ministry** for the purpose of teaching stewardship principles to fellow believers. This business model was going to be different. Dayspring was created to present live workshops about stewardship at no cost to the church or the participants. My knowledge of personal finance and tax laws would join together to create a program about how to manage wealth in God's way, and how to take advantage of legal ways to reduce taxes owed. The reduced tax bills would allow for more giving, savings, and paying off debt. To cover the costs of running the Dayspring website, as well as the travel expenses to churches hosting the workshops, there would be a modest charge for individual coaching. To make sure that anyone who needed counseling could get it, free and reduced-price counseling was to be made available too.

This book began as a supplement to the information taught at the workshop. For those taking the workshop, it acts as a reinforcement. For those not near one of the live workshops, the book is, I hope, a resource they can use to learn biblical stewardship principles. Financial counseling is available to anyone, anywhere, regardless of whether they attended a workshop or not. I'm excited to see where God will take this ministry. If you find it of value for your own stewardship walk, please share it with your friends, family, and coworkers. When dealing with something as personal as their finances, word of mouth is the best advertising!

Thank you for being a part of this ministry. Now, on to the Steward Plan!

John A. Madison, CPA, CRPC, AWMA
john@dayspringfm.com
www.dayspringfm.com

CHAPTER 1

THE CAPITALIST CHRISTIAN

The America in which we reside today has changed dramatically since our founding over 240 years ago. Many of these changes, of course, have been for the better. In many respects, the United States of America remains the shining city upon a hill spoken of in Ronald Reagan's farewell address in 1989 (*The New York Times* 1989). We are still, for better or worse, the desired destination for millions striving for a better life for themselves and their family. But is the America they find today one that is, at least economically, the same as the one found by earlier generations of immigrants? Would a child born in America today have the same economic opportunities experienced by their predecessors?

Capitalism—an economic system in which ownership of the means, distribution, and exchange of wealth is controlled by private individuals and corporations versus the government (Dictionary.com n.d.)—has been under assault in America. In fairness, some of the criticism is well deserved. There have been multiple high-profile cases of individuals or companies taking unfair advantage of consumers, competitors, or investors. Capitalism, like every other economic system, can be abused. Greed and corruption are possible in all systems whether capitalist, communist, or socialist. What is indisputable, however, is that the standard of living and upward economic mobility is the greatest in capitalist systems.

Unfortunately, many in our society today espouse the belief that achieving financial success surely means that you are selfish and greedy, having profited unfairly from a dishonest system. Interestingly, many of those same people are advocates of a robust public education system, from preschool to subsidized college programs, presumably to prepare one for a successful career. So, is it acceptable to prepare for success but then wrong to actually succeed?

Should a Christian Be Financially Successful?

Due primarily to a relatively few manipulators and abusers of the American capitalist system, the idea of achieving financial success has become tarnished in the eyes of many. These concerns are often multiplied in the Christian community. The obvious material poverty during the earthly ministry of Jesus Christ has incorrectly led many believers, as well as many critics of Christianity, to believe that material wealth runs counter to Christ's lifestyle. A 2011 study found that, "Overall, more Americans believe that Christian values are at odds with capitalism and the free market than believe they are compatible. This pattern also holds among Christians. Among Christians in the U.S., only 38% believe capitalism and the free market are consistent with Christian values while 46% believe the two are at odds" (Cox and Jones 2011). As practicing Christians who strive for "Christ-likeness" in our lives, are we to also be destitute?

While Christ certainly warned His listeners about the dangers of undue importance placed upon one's financial condition, neither He nor God condemned wealth or success in our career. The apostle Paul wrote in 1 Timothy 6:10 (NKJV), "For the *love* of money is a root of all kinds of evil, for which some have strayed from the faith in their greediness, and pierced themselves through with many sorrows." While this verse is often seen as a warning to those of financial means, it applies equally to those of limited (or no) wealth whose focus is on what they do not have, or upon an improper belief that wealth will lead to happiness and contentment. The *love* of money is a sin that is not limited to certain income or wealth levels.

Financial success in the career of a Christian should not be seen as ungodly. God expects us to work hard and honestly. Psalm 90:17 (NKJV) calls on God to "establish the work of our hands." Proverbs 12:11 states, "Those who work their land will have abundant food." Proverbs 14:23: "All hard work brings a profit, but mere talk leads only to poverty." God's guidance is given to both genders as well. The virtuous wife in Proverbs 31 is praised when she "makes linen garments and sells them, and supplies the merchants with sashes." Should God grant a believer financial success, then God should be praised and we should rejoice for our brother or sister in Christ, not judge them harshly or be jealous of their success.

Core Beliefs for Christian Personal Finance

What are the core beliefs that should serve as a foundation to a Christian's wealth goals and management? How should a believer view personal finance? And how do we execute those beliefs in practical, real-life steps?

First, believers should always remember that God owns everything, at all times. "Indeed, heaven and the highest heavens belong to the Lord your God, also the earth with all that is in it" (Deuteronomy 10:14 NKJV). Genesis 1:26 (NKJV) (among other verses) specifically states that mankind is to have dominion (or control) over "all the earth," but it does *not* state that God cedes ownership to us. We are only temporary stewards of any wealth we may possess. Eventually, everything we own will either be owned by someone else (property, money in the bank or invested in stocks or bonds) or used in full and of no future value (food, clothing).

As stewards, Christians are to manage the resources we control in a manner that is pleasing to the true owner, God, and consistent with His principles. He expects us to be consistently trustworthy in our management of His wealth. 1 Corinthians 4:2 (NKJV) states, "Moreover it is required in stewards that one be found faithful." That doesn't mean, though, that we're to live as paupers, never enjoying the resources He's laid before us. In fact, it's quite the opposite.

As any good father would, He wants us to enjoy our lives and the blessings He has given to us. That would include using a portion of our wealth not just for the bare minimum living standards, but also to enjoy the fruits of our labor. The key requirements, though, are to never lose sight of who the true owner is and to never look to our possessions for meaning and contentment. Our relationship with Christ is the most important and should always retain that vital position in our lives.

Second Timothy 3:16 (NKJV) states that "All Scripture *is* given by inspiration of God, and *is* profitable for doctrine, for reproof, for correction, for instruction in righteousness." The instructions given in the Scripture cover many areas of our day-to-day spiritual and physical life. Thus, it comes as no surprise that the Bible is overflowing with verses concerning the use of money and the place it should (and should not) play in our lives. Every verse is included by God's design and is important in its own right. However, to prevent this book from being thousands of pages long, the scriptural references have been culled to a more manageable list of verses. It's important to note, though, that none of the excluded verses contradict the financial principles discussed throughout this book. It is from these verses that we find the stewardship steps He expects from us as the manager of His resources.

The *STEWARD* Plan for a Christian's Personal Finances

In order to simplify the steps a steward should take in managing God's wealth, we can follow the *STEWARD* Plan. By addressing each of the personal financial areas covered by the seven letters of the acronym, a steward can create a comprehensive and biblically compliant plan.

Care should be taken to address each of the seven areas listed below and detailed in subsequent chapters. While each is independent of the others, they work together to create a full, comprehensive financial plan.

The *STEWARD* Plan

Set financial goals (Chapter 2) – As the expression goes (commonly attributed to Benjamin Franklin), "Failing to plan is planning to fail." What would God have you to achieve with your personal finances? Are you placing your goals above His goals for you?

For where your treasure is,
there your heart will be also.

MATTHEW 6:21

Tithe cheerfully (Chapter 3) – We give out of obedience and recognition that all we have is His anyway. But are we doing so cheerfully and willingly?

As soon as the commandment was circulated, the
children of Israel brought in abundance the firstfruits
of grain and wine, oil and honey, and of all the
produce of the field; and they brought in
abundantly the tithe of everything.

2 CHRONICLES 31:5 (NKJV)

Establish a spending plan (Chapter 4) – Here, the steward lays out the spending plan each month to maximize the benefit of each available dollar toward meeting their financial goals. Money not given a specific purpose tends to disappear with no awareness of where it went.

Suppose one of you wants to build a tower.
Won't you first sit down and estimate the cost to
see if you have enough money to complete it?

LUKE 14:28

Wipe out consumer debt (Chapter 5) – Few things can hinder long-term financial success and wealth building more than consumer debt.

> *Owe no one anything, except to love*
> *each other, for the one who loves*
> *another has fulfilled the law.*

ROMANS 13:8 (ESV)

Accumulate diversified wealth over time (Chapter 6) – Building wealth usually takes time. Certainly, God's Word cautions believers against pursuing quick gains at the expense of our walk with Him. So, what are some investing principles we should follow?

> *Invest in seven ventures, yes, in*
> *eight; you do not know what disaster*
> *may come upon the land.*

ECCLESIASTES 11:2

Remove unnecessary risk (Chapter 7) – Even the best, most biblically solid plans can be undermined and destroyed by retaining risk that should have been eliminated.

> *The prudent see danger and take ref-*
> *uge, but the simple keep going and*
> *pay the penalty.*

PROVERBS 27:12

Develop an estate plan (Chapter 8) – Scripture counsels believers to plan not only for our immediate needs, but also the needs of future generations. We should be generationally minded with our financial management.

A good person leaves an inheritance
for their children's children, but a
sinner's wealth is stored up for the
righteous.

PROVERBS 13:22

The balance of this book describes and explains each of these important areas of Christian personal financial stewardship, with one chapter for each topic. While it's impossible to cover every possible scenario for these steps, the next chapters will, I hope, begin to help you understand the principle to be applied to your financial lives.

A Word of Encouragement as We Get Started

While we must constantly make important decisions about our finances, the most important of all is to adopt the mindset of a steward. Every financial decision we make should be viewed from that perspective. When I managed the business assets of my accounting clients, I never viewed them as my assets—I was a steward of *their* wealth and always made decisions that were in their best interest, not mine. Surely, all would agree that was the proper perspective and we all would desire that stewards of our assets behave in that manner. Likewise, God expects the same of us with the management of His wealth!

There is nothing magical about the steps recommended throughout this book. Most would be considered common sense. Further, there are no guarantees that your decisions will end up being right when viewed in hindsight, regardless of how closely you follow the guidelines contained in **The STEWARD Plan**. We've all made money mistakes in the past and will in the future too.

God doesn't expect perfection in our stewardship any more than He expects us to be sinless after salvation. What He does want, in every aspect of our lives (including financial stewardship), is a heart that loves Him, places Him above all else, and sincerely commits to following Him. If we can do this, we need not worry about the financial decisions we have to make. Whether they turn out to be good or (in hindsight) not-so-good decisions, He knows our heart and our love for Him. That is, in my opinion, the very essence of being the *"good and faithful servant"* (Matthew 25:21) that He desires from each of us.

While I don't know what will happen to me in my remaining time here on Earth, I know my eternity is secure. As a Christian, I have placed my faith in Jesus Christ alone and I accept the promises He has made to cleanse my sin and welcome me to Heaven at the appointed time. Surely, if I trust God with my eternal soul, I can trust Him with my checkbook too.

CHAPTER 2

SET FINANCIAL GOALS

For where your treasure is, there your heart will be also.

MATTHEW 6:21

E ven those of us with a somewhat limited construction background understand the importance of a strong foundation. Before any of the other tradesmen can do their work—the framers, plumbers, electricians, roofers, painters—the foundation has to be designed and properly laid in place. The failure to do this vital first step makes all of the other work useless as no structure will stand for long on a weak—or nonexistent—foundation.

The same holds true for our financial lives. Quite simply, if you don't address some key areas upfront—in other words, lay a solid foundation—your chances of achieving *"financial success"* are greatly diminished.

The foundation for all areas of our lives must always be Jesus Christ alone. His plans for us should be our plans, whether it concerns our finances, our family, our career, or our service for Him. He created us and knows us better than we know ourselves. Our responsibility is to grow in our knowledge of Him, cultivate our relationship with Him in love, and seek out His will in all areas of our lives. Then, as we begin to consider our financial goals, the process will truly be another expression of worship as we seek His will, not our own. As Proverbs 16:3 says, "Commit to the Lord whatever you do, and he will establish your plans."

Beginning the Process

How then do we begin to formulate our financial goals? First, as with everything, begin with prayer. In fact, "pray without ceasing" (1 Thessalonians 5:17 NKJV). This will help center our hearts on Him, not on our worldly material resources. This is a great deterrent to selfishness, which is an all too common human condition.

Next, we need to begin to ponder what to accomplish in our financial lives. Note that it may **not** include the desire to retire with a multimillion-dollar portfolio. Should you be so blessed, great. The Scripture commands us to work. In Genesis 2:15, God directed Adam to tend to (or work, depending on your translation) the Garden *before* the original sin and fall of man. Work is not a punishment, but a gift of God, and it will bring material blessings for some believers. But God may choose, in His wisdom, to bless others for their work in nonmaterial ways.

At this point, simply consider the possibilities. If you're married, include your spouse in the process of determining where God wants you to go. Not only will your individual goals begin to materialize, you may learn a lot about what is important to your spouse along the way. Marriages can be strengthened through this process.

- Do you want to retire early?
- Is God calling you to the mission field?
- Do you want to be able to send your kids to a certain college?
- Do you have a desire to live in a special location, like the beach?
- Would you like to start your own business?

Too often, people start financial goal setting with the numbers and not the *why*. You may have a goal to pay off debt. A fine goal, of course, but why? Is it to allow you to save more? Or to spend more? Or to invest more? Or to have one parent stay home with the kids? Each of these reasons are perfectly valid, but may require a different process to achieve.

Saving more is a great goal too. But again, why? Is it to retire early? To pay for an expensive anniversary trip? To pay for your children's college expenses? Or to move to part-time work so you can spend more time on a spiritual calling? Again, different reasons often mean different processes.

The first step is to simply talk and to dream. It's not to get out a spreadsheet and work on the spending plan or debt elimination strategies or types of investments.

Getting Started

If you haven't tried financial goal setting before, it can be intimidating. Where do I start? Here are some areas to discuss and prayerfully consider:

- **Where are you now?** No sugar-coating and no ignoring the problems. What is working and perhaps more importantly, what is not? You can't begin to fix a problem until you admit it exists. And you can't eliminate the problem until you're honest about its depth. Remember the admonition in Proverbs 27:23 (NKJV): "Be diligent to know the state of your flocks, and attend to your herds." Be real about the good and the bad.

- **Who is determining your goals for the future?** How do you decide your goals in life, not just financially, but in all areas? Do you decide your objective and then ask God to bless it? If your goal isn't part of His plan for you, you may not like the reply you receive from your prayer. Then you're left with feeling disappointed and even bitter toward God for Him not endorsing your plan or, I suppose, you could go for it anyway, but I'm sure we both know how that would end up! Instead, heed Proverbs 16:3 quoted earlier. As a reminder, this verse states, "Commit to the Lord whatever you do, and he will establish your plans."

Don't miss this! First and foremost, *decide to live God's plan for your life (whatever it may be)*, then let Him bring ideas to your mind and life that move you toward His goals for you. Remember His promise in Jeremiah 29:11, which states, "'For I know the plans I have for you,' declares the LORD, 'plans to prosper you and not to harm you, plans to give you hope and a future.'" These are goals we can trust are for our good!

- **What are your goals?** Where does God want you to be five, ten years from now? As the saying goes, "If you aim at nothing, you'll hit it every time." What are you aiming for? If you're married, are you on the same page with your spouse? Or do you have radically different goals? Disharmony in a godly marriage may be a sign that one, or both parties, are pursuing their goals instead of God's. Remember to keep Him first and look for Him (in His timing) to formulate ideas and circumstances in your life to point you toward the goals in your life, including financial. Stay flexible. Remember the assurance found in Proverbs 3:5 and 6: "Trust in the LORD with all your heart, and lean not on your own understanding; in all your ways submit to him, and He will make your paths straight." He may not reveal the entire plan in advance, so as you're contemplating financial goals, understand that they may (and probably will) change over time.

- **What are you willing to sacrifice to meet your goals?** No one really wants to talk about sacrifice, but it's usually part of the process. If you want to lose weight, you may have to "sacrifice" dessert. If you want a new career, you may have to "sacrifice" some time to attain the required education and build a network in a new industry. To succeed financially (remember: success is defined by attaining God's will for your finances), you may have to "sacrifice" the deluxe cable TV package or eating out for lunch every weekday. Or you may need to drive your existing car for another year or two. But think how much easier it is to make these sacrifices when you have a goal—the true reason—in mind. Sacrifice simply for the sake of sacrifice is painful and seems pointless. Sacrifice for the sake of meeting your higher priority goal is part of living victoriously. The discomfort is a reminder that you're one step closer to meeting your objective.

These aren't questions easily answered (at least not accurately) in one brief discussion. They take time to fully answer, but it is time well spent. God will reveal more to us as we remain in Him and in His word. So be patient and always alert to His conviction to add, delete, or alter a financial goal. Remember: a solid foundation in Christ leads to the development of effective strategies, which—when implemented successfully—lead to financial success.

Only you can answer the questions posed earlier (and others as well) that deal with your financial goals in life. Few things are sadder than to work for decades toward a goal that is unsatisfying when it's achieved! I was blessed to be able to retire from full-time accounting work at the age of forty-nine, but I had focused so intently on my career that I never took the time to prayerfully consider what God would have me to do with the additional time I'd have available.[1] Take the time now to understand the destination (or at least the possibilities) before you begin the journey.

Over time, these dreams can (and most likely will) change as your life evolves. That is perfectly fine. We're defining the goals in pencil, not etching them in stone.

What will you choose?

In October 1964, Ronald Reagan delivered a speech entitled "A Time for Choosing" in support of the ultimately doomed Barry Goldwater presidential campaign. The crux of the speech was that America was at a crossroads and needed to decide which of two paths it was to follow:

---

[1] After several years of frustrating starts and stops with various potential projects, I felt led to start Dayspring Financial Ministry to volunteer my time and knowledge to teach biblical stewardship. Better prayerful planning may have avoided the time lost to uncertainty for my "encore" career!

conservative or progressive. Lyndon Johnson's landslide victory the next month clearly demonstrated the choice America made. However, sixteen years later, Reagan himself was elected president as America decided to change the path it previously chose.

In our financial lives, we sometimes face a time of choosing as well. We may find ourselves in a challenging situation not of our own making. The possibilities are endless: an unexpected job loss; a negative medical diagnosis resulting in large, unpaid bills; financial infidelity by our spouse. Or the financial problems could be a result of our own poor choices. Regardless of the genesis of the problem, we face a choice. Do we remain in the mess, blaming life or God or someone else for our predicament? Or do we choose to take a path leading us to greener pastures? The choice isn't always as easy as it sounds as our human nature often derives some comfort from our ills. Will you face the stark reality of your financial situation and devise a plan to escape? Or will you stay mired in the problems, blaming "the man" and feeling certain that "the little guy (or girl) can't get ahead"?

In the Bible, the apostle Paul asked God three times to remove a "thorn in his side." Scriptures don't define the thorn. Some say it was a physical ailment. Others suggest it was a demon, or perhaps a group of critics who followed and heckled him. Regardless of what it was, God's answer was always the same. "No," God said. "My grace is sufficient." Therefore, Paul faced a time of choosing—focus on the thorn or focus on something greater than his situation. He chose the latter and became the greatest missionary of all time.

Is this a time for choosing in your financial life? What choice will you make? Will it be to follow God's stewardship guidance or our own judgment?

CHAPTER 3

TITHE CHEERFULLY

As soon as the commandment was circulated, the children of Israel brought in abundance the firstfruits of grain and wine, oil and honey, and of all the produce of the field; and they brought in abundantly the tithe of everything.

2 Chronicles 31:5 (NKJV)

Imagine you are gathering with your family to celebrate Christmas. A beautifully decorated tree stands in the corner of the room with twinkling lights and presents galore underneath. A crackling fire warms the room as Christmas music plays softly in the background. The aroma of the just finished meal still floats throughout the room. Your family members, young and old alike, join together to exchange presents in a show of love and affection for one another. One by one, presents are handed to the excited recipients who anxiously await the opportunity to open a gift lovingly chosen for them.

Finally, when your turn arrives, a gift is placed in your lap. You open the attached card first and it says, "I know I'm supposed to give you something since it's Christmas. So, here's a gift. My duty is done for the year." How would you feel? Was the gift given in love or obligation?

Cheerful Giving

All too often, many Christians approach tithing with such an attitude, even if it's unintended. Obedience is important, they believe, so we give "our" money to the church because we're commanded to do so. But is that truly the command?

Certainly, we are to give to God's work. Proverbs 3:9 (NKJV) states, "Honor the Lord with your possessions, and with the firstfruits of all your increase." The giving of the firstfruits funds the church from a practical perspective, but more importantly, it's an outward acknowledgement that all we have is really God's. He blessed us with the ability to work, so even the paycheck we "earned" is really His. Deuteronomy 8:18 begins, "But remember the LORD your God, for it is he who gives you the ability to produce wealth."

More important than simply meeting some financial obligation, God looks to our hearts. Are we giving out of love for Him? Or out of obligation like the earlier story? The Scripture presents in no uncertain terms how we are to give: "Each of you should give what you have decided in your heart to give, not reluctantly or under compulsion, for God loves a cheerful giver" (2 Corinthians 9:7). Should you find yourself giving out of obligation, prayerfully reconsider your motives. Give in love, not grudgingly. With the right mental approach, we are blessed as we see God use our tithes and offerings to save souls and work wonders.

Be One of the Few

Unfortunately, statistics show that few Christians tithe. Among Christians overall, only 2% tithe (NP Source 2018), which is defined as giving 10% ("one-tenth") of one's income. Further, the trend is declining over time as, unfortunately, more Americans no longer identify with any religion (The Giving Institute 2015). Today's Christians are only giving 2.5% of their income. For perspective, during the Great Depression, Christians were giving 3.3%. Here are some more disappointing tithing statistics as of 2018 (NP Source 2018):

- Only 3–5% of Americans who give to their local church do so through regular tithing.
- Interestingly, when surveyed, 17% of Americans state that they regularly tithe.
- For families making $75,000 or more, only 1% of them gave at least 10%.
- 37% of regular church attendees and Evangelicals don't give money to church.

While the statistics are disheartening, we can choose a different path for our financial priorities. And it begins with the firstfruits, tithing to your local church.

Should you find your current financial situation to be dire and there appears to be no room in your budget to tithe, accept the challenge God laid out in Malachi. In Malachi 3:10 (NKJV), we find the only instance that God is calling us to test Him. "'Bring all the tithes into the storehouse, that there may be food in My house, and try Me now in this,' says the LORD of hosts, 'If I will not open for you the windows of heaven and pour out for you *such* blessing that there *will* not *be* room enough to *receive it*." Our Father owns "the cattle on a thousand hills" (Psalm 50:10) and He stands prepared to bless us for cheerfully trusting Him with our tithe.

It is important to note, however, that this is not a promise to make us rich if we tithe. It is a promise to "bless" us. Those blessings may come in the form of financial gain, or they may be in some other form. What is important is that we cheerfully give to Him, He receives it and will in turn bless us in a manner He sees fit. Regardless of the form it takes, we can be sure that His blessing will exceed our expectations. Truly, the giver of the gift (tithe) becomes the recipient.

How to Get to 10%

Many of my clients are struggling financially even before they consider tithing. Perhaps you are in this situation too. One can reasonably ask, "If I'm living paycheck to paycheck without tithing, how can I afford to tithe?"

Always remember the challenge from God in Malachi 3:10 mentioned earlier. Test Him. He's asking you to do so! Here are two ideas that may help. First, when you budget, make the tithe the *first* expenditure listed, not the last one (If there is any money left by then!). If your situation is too dire, then simply begin to give what you can to your local church. Maybe it's only 1% or 2% of your income. Slowly increase the amount over time, or perhaps do so when you get the next raise or you pay off a debt. I can't explain God's ways. But I do hold on to His promises. Commit to giving and start today. He'll handle the math!

The Tithing Question

So, what is *the* tithing question that has vexed Christians around the world for generation after generation?

Answer: Whether Christians should tithe off of their **gross** or **net** income! Kidding aside, the study mentioned earlier found that seven out of ten tithers do so based on their gross and not their net income (NP Source 2018). For what it's worth, my wife and I tithe based on our gross income. We are instructed to give our first fruits to God, not our "net" fruits! I've never seen in the Scripture where taxes paid (no matter how much) are excluded from your "increase" for the year. Money was also spent for food, for example, but that was still a part of your income for the year. Taxes are just an expenditure like any other (even though it's removed from your paycheck before you actually receive it).

This certainly isn't a salvation issue. God's going to fervently love you whether you tithe or not. All I can suggest is this: examine the Scripture and prayerfully consider what God would have you do. With only 3% to 5% currently giving, the issue isn't whether it should be off of gross or net; it's not being done by the vast majority of believers anyway. Remember: handling money in God's way can clear the space in your budget to tithe!

Tax-Efficient Tithing Strategies

We should look at our tithes and offerings as worship to God. We do so in recognition that He gave it all to us, and we give cheerfully in obedience and love for God and others. Giving for the singular purpose of potential tax benefits may be a prudent step financially, but it surely would not be an act of worship! This sort of attitude among believers regarding giving is short-sighted. That having been said, good stewardship requires us to manage His assets as well as possible, and this would include knowing the basics of our tax laws to pay as little tax as legally possible.

Our current tax laws present us with several strategies that may provide the giver with larger tax benefits than simply writing a check each week or month to contribute your tithe to the local church. These strategies may also apply to other charitable giving you may complete throughout the year. As we'll also see, the significant changes to the tax laws in 2017 (that applied starting in 2018) made these strategies even more valuable.

Romans 13:7 (NKJV) begins, "Render therefore to all their due: taxes to whom taxes are due…." Clearly, we are required by the Scripture to pay the proper amount of tax as determined by the laws of our government, whether we like the tax rules or not. I am as frustrated as any American when I read news reports of the rampant fraud, waste, and abuse throughout the various levels of government. But there is no provision in the Scripture to justify paying any less than what we actually owe per these laws.

However, structuring our financial affairs in such a way to minimize the legal amount of taxes paid is endorsed by our government. In the 1935 case before the US Supreme Court (Gregory v. Helvering), the majority opinion included the statement, "The legal right of a taxpayer to decrease the amount of what otherwise would be his [or her] taxes, or altogether avoid them, by means which the law permits, cannot be doubted." Translation: Structuring your financial affairs in a way that **complies with the law** and at the same time minimizes or eliminates your tax liability is the law of the land. Therefore, we can utilize these giving strategies to reduce our tax burden and still fully comply with the Scripture command given us in Romans 13:7.

Note: The strategies discussed are in compliance with current federal tax law at the time of writing. Changes may have occurred in the law between then and when you are reading about them. Please make sure you understand any changes. Also, state tax laws are not taken into consideration in the discussion of the strategies as each state is different. Please consult a tax advisor familiar with the laws in your state before implementing any of these strategies.

Strategy 1 – Donating Appreciated Securities

Assumptions for this strategy:

1. Investment assets (stocks, bonds, mutual funds, ETFs) are owned in a nonretirement brokerage account.
2. These assets have been owned for over one year.
3. The current market value for these assets is higher than when they were purchased (in other words, there are unrealized gains in the holdings).

Application of the strategy: Federal tax law allows for the **fair market value** (FMV) of a donated security to be the amount of the donor's itemized deduction, if the above conditions are met. The FMV is used instead of the original cost of the security and the gain you earned since you purchased the security is never taxed. The example below will explain this better.

Discussion of the strategy: The best way to understand this strategy is with an example.

- Noah purchased 100 shares of Ark Building Company, Inc. (ticker symbol ARK), a publicly traded company on January 2, 2015 for $20 per share—total cost: $2,000.
- As of January 21, 2019, the shares of ARK trade for $80 per share, so Noah's holding is worth $8,000.
- Noah would like to donate $8,000 to his church.
- Assume that Noah is in a 30% income tax bracket and a 20% capital gains bracket.

If Noah sells the shares for $8,000, he will realize a gain of $6,000 (sales price: $8,000 less; purchase price: $2,000 equals a long-term capital gain of $6,000). His tax on this capital gain would be: $6,000 times 20% capital gains rate, or $1,200. After paying the tax, Noah has $6,800 remaining (sales proceeds of $8,000 less the capital gains tax paid of $1,200). He can donate the $6,800 to the church along with another $1,200 of other money to reach his donation goal of $8,000.

Assume that, instead of selling the stock, Noah donates the shares of ARK to his church. As we read in the application note above, he will be credited with making a donation of $8,000 (the fair market value of the shares donated). As he donated the shares instead of selling them, there is no sale, so he will not owe any capital gains tax! The church will immediately sell the shares of ARK and receive the $8,000 in proceeds. As the church is a nonprofit, they will not have to pay tax on the capital gain.

With either of these options, the church received $8,000 in value and Noah is entitled to an $8,000 charitable deduction, taken as a part of his itemized deductions. However, he had to pay $1,200 in capital gains tax in the first scenario, but zero capital gains tax in the second one.

With the change in the tax law (via the **Tax Cut and Jobs Act of 2017**), there was a dramatic increase in the amount of the standard deduction for all filing status. Therefore, significantly fewer taxpayers will be itemizing under the new rules. With that in mind, does it still make sense for Noah to donate appreciated securities if he is *not* going to itemize?

The answer is yes! Even though he may take the standard deduction and thus not deduct the contribution, he still avoids the capital gains tax owed in the first scenario.

Strategy 2 – Establish a Donor Advised Fund

Assumptions for this strategy (the first three are the same as Strategy 1):

1. Investment assets (stocks, bonds, mutual funds, ETFs) are owned in a nonretirement brokerage account.
2. These assets have been owned for over one year.
3. The current market value for these assets is higher than when they were purchased (in other words, there are unrealized gains in the holdings).
4. You'd like to spread the donations to: (1) multiple charities, and/or (2) throughout the year (or multiple years).

Application of the strategy: Instead of donating appreciated securities directly to the charity (Strategy 1 – Donating Appreciated Securities), set up a Donor Advised Fund (DAF) to receive the appreciated securities, and then recommend grants from the DAF to the church or charity when you'd like (even over multiple years).

Discussion of the strategy: Strategy 1 presents taxpayers with tremendous potential tax benefits. However, there are a couple of limiting factors: (1) the charity has to be in the position to receive the appreciated securities (many are not); and (2) they have immediate access to the full donation, even if you prefer to spread it out over multiple months or years. The Donor Advised Fund (DAF) helps eliminate these factors.

The DAF is a charitable organization itself. They are designed to be able to receive appreciated securities, sell them after receipt, invest the money while it is in the DAF, then receive grant recommendations and make distributions to the recommended charities (if approved). Think of the DAF as simply an intermediary between the donor (you) and the ultimate charity you wish to bless (for example, your church). The DAF was set up to specifically handle donations of this type, making the donating process much easier for the donor and the ultimate donee.

Donations made to the DAF are irrevocable and the donor receives a tax deduction (like Strategy 1) for the FMV of the donated securities. While the DAF technically controls and owns the donated funds, the original donor retains the ability to "recommend a grant" to a qualified charity. Assuming the charity is qualified, the DAF will act on the grant recommendation and contribute funds as specified in the grant request. The donor does not receive a deduction for this part of the transaction as they received it when they put the funds into the DAF.

A few advantages of using a DAF are:

- A DAF simplifies the process for giving appreciated securities.
- The donor receives an immediate tax deduction for the FMV of the securities contributed, even if it takes multiple years for the DAF to distribute the funds.
- A DAF can offer anonymity for the donor, if so desired.
- The donor's gross estate value is lower, potentially saving estate taxes and bypassing the probate process for those assets.
- Future growth by the funds in the DAF are tax free.
- Use of DAF simplifies "itemized expense bunching," a strategy that will be more popular under the new tax law.

"Itemized Expense Bunching" Explained

"Itemized expense bunching" is, at its core, a strategy that pushes as many tax deductions as possible in one tax year to exceed the standard deduction and allow for itemizing. The other year(s), the taxpayer will have lower itemized deductions and will instead use the standard deduction. An illustration will make this clearer.

Assume Abraham and Sarah, a married couple filing jointly, have the following potential deductions:

- State and local income, personal property, and real estate taxes (SALT) of $15,000.
- Mortgage interest of $8,000.
- Contributions to their church of $5,000.

They also have a mutual fund in a brokerage account that is worth $10,000 that they purchased three years ago for $2,500.

Without the DAF: Their itemized deductions will be:

- SALT: $10,000 (The 2017 tax law now limits this deduction to $10,000 per year.)
- Mortgage interest: $8,000
- Contributions: $5,000
- Total itemized deductions: $23,000

Since the standard deduction for their filing status is $24,400 (in 2019), they would elect to use the higher standard deduction. They could donate ½ of the mutual fund in their brokerage account to their church each year and avoid the capital gain taxes that would be due if they sold the shares and donated cash (this is another example of Strategy 1).

Assuming their numbers were the same for next year, their two-year deduction total would be $48,800 (the $24,400 standard deduction for year one and year two).

With the DAF: Assume they donated the entire $10,000 in the mutual fund to the DAF in year one. Their year one itemized deductions would be:

- SALT: $10,000 (limited to $10,000 in the 2017 tax law)
- Mortgage interest: $8,000
- Contributions: $10,000 (the donation to the DAF)
- Total itemized deductions: $28,000

Since the $28,000 in itemized deductions is more than the $24,400 standard deduction, they would use the higher itemized figure for their tax return. In year two, their itemized deductions (assuming everything stayed the same) would only be $18,000 (the SALT of $10,000 and the mortgage interest of $8,000; they have no contributions in year two as they donated it all in year one to the DAF). Therefore, they would take the standard deduction in year two, bringing their two-year deduction total to $52,400 ($28,000 year one + $24,400 year two).

Note that by using the DAF, their total deductions for the two-year period was $3,600 more than without using the DAF. Further, with the DAF, they can have a portion of the fund sent to their church each month over the two-year period, allowing their church to have a more steady and predictable income stream. Under both scenarios, Abraham and Sarah's church received $5,000 each year.

Strategy 3 – Qualified Charitable Distributions (QCD)

Assumptions for this strategy:

1. Investment assets are being held in a tax-preferenced account like a 401k, 403b, 457, IRA, Keough, or other similar type of account.
2. The account owner is at least 70 ½ years old and therefore subject to required minimum distributions (RMDs) discussed below.
3. The account owner is charitably inclined and would like to donate money to his church and/or other charities each year.

Application of the strategy: Instead of receiving (and paying tax on) RMDs each year, the RMD is contributed directly to a qualified charity, satisfying the RMD requirement but not incurring income tax on the distribution.

Discussion on the strategy: No discussion of Qualified Charitable Distributions (QCD) is complete without first discussing Required

Minimum Distributions (RMD). RMDs are the means by which Congress mandates removal of a portion of tax-preferred accounts each year. Generally speaking, once the account owner turns 70 ½ years old, they must take a set percentage of their account balance out of the IRA/401k/403b, etc. each year (Note: there are some exceptions to this general statement, so please speak to an advisor about your situation). When the RMD is removed, it becomes a "taxable event" and the account owner must claim the RMD as income on his/her tax return for the year.

Since an assumption for this strategy is that the account owner is charitably inclined, he/she will also be donating funds to a charity each year. These donations are deductible if the account owner is still itemizing deductions. As discussed earlier, with the higher standard deductions found in the new tax law, only a small percentage of taxpayers will continue to itemize. Therefore, while the donor has to claim the RMD as income, they may not get a corresponding charitable deduction.

Further, the increased income due to the RMD can also impact other areas of the account owners' taxes. These "stealth taxes" can appear in places such as:

- A higher percentage of their Social Security being subject to income tax
- Higher Medicare Parts B and D premiums (as they are means tested—the more you make, the higher your premiums).
- Loss of deductions/credits that are phased out if your income is too high, such as medical expenses and education tax credits.
- The loss of passive loss deductions (from, for example, rental real estate).
- Increased exposure to the 3.8% surtax on net investment income.[2]
- Loss of the ability to contribute to a Roth IRA if the taxpayer is still working.

---

[2] This is an additional tax imposed by the Affordable Care Act ("Obamacare") on certain types of income (such as interest, dividends, capital gains, and rental income). It only applies if your income is above certain limits, which the RMD may result in. For more information, please see: https://www.irs.gov/taxtopics/tc559.

The bottom line is this: Eliminating the RMD from your taxable income may produce a lower tax liability than the alternative of claiming the RMD as income with a corresponding charitable deduction.

Enter the QCD: Instead of receiving the RMD from the IRA custodian, the account holder will request that the custodian send the RMD (or a portion thereof) directly to a charity as a QCD. This would satisfy the RMD requirement (in part or in whole) for the year and the account holder does not have to report the distribution as income. This will lower their Adjusted Gross Income (AGI), the amount on which many of the "stealth taxes" described above are calculated, potentially creating other tax savings.

Of course, since the contribution came from the IRA (for example) and not the account holder personally, there is no deductible contribution for the account holder. Remember, though, that the vast majority of tax payers won't itemize anyway, effectively costing them nothing! Even if they do still itemize, they are no worse off without the additional donation as they also avoided having to claim the RMD as income.

Simple QCD Example

Let's look at a simple QCD example to see the impact.

Assume that Adam and Eve are a married couple filing a joint return and both are over 70 ½ years old. Their RMD for the year is $10,000. Their other income includes:

- Social Security income of $24,000.
- Part-time work of $12,000.
- Pension income of $18,000.

Therefore, their total income, including the RMD, is $64,000. We'll assume for simplicity that they use the standard deduction ($27,000 in 2019, which includes the extra deduction due to their ages).

Without the QCD, their AGI would include the part-time work ($12,000), pension income ($18,000), a portion of their Social Security income ($5,000[3]), and their RMD ($10,000) for a total of $45,000. Their standard deduction ($27,000) reduces the AGI to a taxable income of $18,000. The tax (in 2019) on this amount of taxable income is $1,800.

Suppose instead that they **use the QCD**. The entire $10,000 RMD is given to a qualified charity. Therefore, their AGI is made up of only their part-time work ($12,000) and their pension income ($18,000). None of their Social Security is taxed as the elimination of the RMD reduced their AGI to a level low enough to avoid the requirement to claim any of it. Their new AGI ($30,000) is reduced by the standard deduction ($27,000), which results in a taxable income of $3,000. The tax on this amount is $300 or $1,500 less than shown above (without using a QCD).

Other QCD Considerations / Requirements

- QCDs are only allowed for IRAs, not workplace plans like 401ks or 403bs. If you still have a 401k balance at a prior employer, simply transfer it to an IRA and you will be eligible to complete a QCD.
- The gift must be directly from the IRA to the charity. You cannot receive the distribution and then pay the charity to qualify for a QCD.
- There is a limit of $100,000 per person per year.
- The donor cannot receive anything in return, even a "thank you" tote bag!
- The QCD will not be coded as such on the 1099-R sent the next year. Be sure to tell your tax preparer that it was a QCD to avoid erroneously claiming it as income.
- QCDs cannot be sent to Donor Advised Funds (Strategy 2) or private charities.

---

[3] Social Security is taxed based on how much other income a taxpayer has. For this example, the taxable portion of their Social Security income is $5,000. Consult a tax advisor to determine the amount of your Social Security income that would be taxed, if any.

- The QCD must be the first dollars out of your IRA in a tax year. The first dollars distributed are always considered to be the RMD. So, if you've already taken the full RMD for the current year, you cannot do a QCD this year (for that portion of the RMD).

As noted earlier, be sure to check the current tax rules to verify that these strategies are still available.

Closing Thoughts

Paying the lowest, legal amount of taxes is our right as taxpayers and our requirement as a Christian steward. Utilizing tax-reducing strategies like these can allow a believer to use these savings to pay off debt, to build wealth, or even better, to increase giving for the furtherance of His Kingdom.

Will you make tithing the priority in your spending?
Do you trust God enough to test Him as He calls us to do?
Show you do by returning the tithe to the Giver of all we have.

CHAPTER 4

ESTABLISH A SPENDING PLAN

*Suppose one of you wants to build a tower. Won't you first sit
down and estimate the cost to see if you have
enough money to complete it?*

LUKE 14:28

It's unfortunate that many Christians (and non-Christians too) view a spending plan, otherwise known as a budget, as a difficult and daunting task surely to result in preventing us to have any enjoyment in our lives. In actuality, if done correctly, a spending plan is liberating.

The decision people reach regarding budgeting doesn't seem to have a predictable set of traits. Age doesn't seem to be a factor as I've seen both young and "seasoned" people on both sides of the discussion. Economic status doesn't determine one's openness to creating a spending plan either. One could attempt to argue that the wealthy don't need to budget as they have plenty of resources. But are they being a good steward of whatever riches they are managing? How would they know without a measuring stick to which to compare their actual spending?

A 2013 Gallup poll showed that only 32% of Americans prepare a monthly budget (Jacobe 2013). Their results show that the lack of budgeting crosses all demographic classes. Across every age, income level, education level, and even political ideology, the results are similar—collectively, Americans are not planning their spending.

Years ago, my wife and I were with the majority as we didn't prepare a formal budget each month. We did have a general idea of our spending, and we stayed within the monthly spending cap we set for our family. But how much was spent on food or clothing or eating out or entertainment? We had no idea and I wasn't sure at that time that it even mattered to me.

However, I kept reading about the wisdom and benefit of having a monthly spending plan. The Scripture instructed us to plan our spending in advance (Luke 14:28). So, we decided to start creating a plan each month and the results were shocking. When we saw how we were spending money—and how it often didn't match up to our goals—we quickly changed our spending patterns. And because our new spending plan was more closely aligned to what was important for us, the spending "cuts" weren't painful at all. Giving up something that was less important to achieve goals that are much more important isn't a sacrifice at all—it's being a good steward.

Benefits of Budgeting

Here are some of the benefits we've seen through creating a spending plan before the month begins and accounting for every dollar of income that month:

- *It helps the natural savers to spend and the natural spenders to save.*

God creates each of us unique. For example, I'm a natural saver, while my wife is a natural spender. Neither of these is "better" than the other. We're simply different, for which I thank God. Without me, my wife may struggle to save. And without her, I'd struggle to have a life. It's through the spending plan we prepare each month that both of our unique needs can be met, without either party feeling left out of the process. I can see in advance where we're able to save and invest. And my wife can see where we're funding some of the activities and goals important to her.

- ***For natural savers like me, a spending plan is liberating!***

Prior to creating our plan each month, I often struggled with spending because I didn't know what we'd miss out on because certain dollars were already spent. The economic term for this is *"opportunity cost."* If the funds were spent, what *couldn't* we then do? What opportunity would it cost us?

Now, if we budget a certain amount for eating out that month (as an example), I know that we can freely use those funds for that purpose and not sacrifice some other opportunity. Why? Because those other spending goals are also built into the plan and funded too. Were it not for the budget process, I would have no way of knowing if that were true or not.

- ***It holds you accountable—to each other, to yourself, and to God.***

As a Christian, I believe that all of the wealth I have is from God. While I earned it, saved it, and invested it, He alone gave me the ability to do so. Eventually, every share of a mutual fund, every dollar in a bank account, and every physical asset (with lasting value) that I own will be the property of someone else. It may stay in my possession for hours, days, years, or decades, but eventually, someone else will possess it. They will then be steward of that item. But until then, God has an expectation that I will manage it in a manner pleasing to Him, which does include spending a portion of it on ourselves for fun and entertainment.

Likewise, if you're married, I believe you have accountability to your spouse in regards to how money is handled. It's not my money or her money—it's our money. We should work together to decide how it's spent or invested, taking the desires of both parties into consideration. Within the spending plan should be "blow" money for each party to spend the way they see fit, with the amount set jointly.

Finally, a spending plan gives us a guide by which we can hold ourselves accountable in regards to our spending. Did I follow the plan we set out in advance? Or did my need for immediate gratification lead me to toss the budget aside and instead make an emotional purchase? The written budget can help prevent this costly mistake.

- ***It helps you meet your long-term—and short-term—goals.***

Many important financial goals can't be fully addressed with one month's income. This is true for both long-term and short-term goals.

Some short-term goals may be:

- to save for an upcoming vacation
- funding the braces your child will need in a few years
- saving for the car that will need to be replaced or a down payment on a new home
- or perhaps giving to an upcoming charitable event that is important to you.

Conversely, your long-term goals may include things like:

- saving for retirement
- saving for your child's college education
- saving for your child's wedding
- buying a vacation home
- being able to move to a rewarding encore career earlier than full retirement age

A spending plan allows you to more easily set aside funds to meet these goals in a timely manner. Could you meet them without a budget? Of course, but it's likely to take much longer to do so. Without the discipline of regularly contributing to these goals, the amount of time required to fund them will be longer, and perhaps cost you the opportunity to meet them.

- *It helps show your bad spending habits.*

All of us have spending weak spots. We're all human and sometimes our natural desire for something leads us to mismanage our resources. A spending plan will shine a light on those areas and give us the opportunity to address them.

- *It increases your financial peace of mind.*

How much more stressful would your vacation be if you simply packed up your family in the car and started driving in a random direction, not sure where you were going or when you'd get there? How could you even pack correctly for the trip? Will you be at the beach or on the ski slopes?

Likewise, how can you gain financial peace of mind without a plan? How much more confident would you be with a fully funded emergency fund (made possible by funding it each month until it was complete)? In Matthew 6:34, we are told, in part, to "not worry about tomorrow." Maybe His plan to deal with this financial worry is for you to obey His advice in Luke 14:28! Don't increase the uncertainty of the future by not preparing for it today.

- *It helps you avoid debt.*

One of the most common causes of debt is from a lack of planning. A broken heat pump can lead to a credit card balance because you didn't budget for funding an emergency fund. A car purchase may include a new car loan because you didn't set aside money each month for the vehicle you knew you'd eventually need. Loans for your child's college education may have to be paid for years after graduation because the money wasn't set aside each month when they were young.

Budget Fears

With all these benefits, why do less than a third of all Americans actually prepare a monthly spending plan? I think a few of the most common reasons are:

35

- **People hear "budget" and think "bread and water."**

Many people don't like the limits they feel a budget will place on them. Understandable but incorrect if a budget is done the right way. This is actually an opportunity to live out the financial side of God's plan for your life.

- **They are afraid of what they'll find.**

Budgeting can be scary at first. You may not want to find out the cost of your latte habit. However, sticking your head in the sand isn't the answer. Knowledge is power. Deal with the truth and move on.

When we first started budgeting, I was shocked to find out how much we were spending on food (both groceries and eating out). No one likes to face cold, hard facts like these, but because we did, we were able to reduce our spending in this area. And truth be told, it really didn't change the quality (or quantity) of food we eat. It just made us more efficient in how we use our food dollars.

- **Budget abuse in the past.**

Some people have used the budget process to abuse others. In reality, the budget was just another tool they used to manipulate and control others.

Unfortunately, a lot of good things have been misused. That doesn't make preparing a budget bad. It just makes the abuser wrong! Don't tarnish the benefits of a budget due to someone misusing it in your past.

- **Pride.**

"I don't need to do a budget! That's for poor people." This is not a biblical mindset. Proverbs 11:2 reminds us, "When pride comes, then comes disgrace, but with humility comes wisdom." Don't let pride lead you to think God's call to make a plan doesn't apply to you. We all have a responsibility to be good stewards of our resources, whether the resources are large or small.

Don't let your financial future be harmed because of your precon-ceived notion about who needs a spending plan. We all do.

- **Laziness.**

Let's be honest. I understand how easy it would be to let budgeting slide. Streaming a movie and a quart of ice cream sounds much better than doing a budget. A lot of people have to fight off laziness each month to get the budget prepared.

Budgeting is like many other processes we do each month. Understanding the benefits and building the habit are the keys. I may feel too lazy to go to the grocery store, but I understand the benefits of eating and I've grown accustomed to it. Now that I've personally experienced the benefits of budgeting, I can't imagine living without it.

Proverbs 12:24 states, "Diligent hands will rule, but laziness ends in forced labor." Don't let laziness derail your stewardship.

- **Don't know how to prepare one.**

Effective budgeting can seem daunting to start. Do I do it on paper or on the computer? How detailed do I need to make the spending catego-ries? How do I handle the irregular expenses?

Here's a suggestion: Don't try to figure it all out before you even get started. Honestly, you won't at first. Start from where you are and just begin. A simple list of things you need to spend money on that equals the amount you have coming in that month is a great beginning. Over time, you can refine it.

Don't let the fear of starting keep you from doing so. You'll never get better until you dive in!

- **Past failures at budgeting.**

Maybe you have tried in the past and it didn't go well. Don't quit—try again! Few really valuable and meaningful things come easy the first time you try. Did you skin your knee learning how to ride a bike? Most of us did. But if you don't get back on the bike, you'll be sitting on the curb watching the other kids have all the fun.

Get back on the budget bike! You learn by doing. Falling off the budget bike is okay. Not getting back on isn't. Remember Galatians 6:9: "Let us not become weary in doing good, for at the proper time we will reap a harvest if we do not give up."

- **It will lead to marital fights.**

I have to be honest. The first few budget meetings I had with my wife didn't go well. We both came into them with our own expectations and they didn't necessarily match up. Part of a great marriage relationship is working together on tough things. It also includes putting our spouse's needs ahead of our own.

Once my wife and I stumbled our way through the first few budgets, we noticed it getting easier and easier. And we noticed that we both found some things to like about the budget. That's what marriage is about—working together to make a better future for ourselves and our families.

- **I'm a free spirit. Budgets are for nerds.**

As a CPA, a thrill for me is a column of numbers that adds up properly. I also understand that a lot of people aren't like me in this regard. They still need to do a budget, though. Remember that the budget isn't designed to squelch their free spirit. It's to let them enjoy some impulsiveness without going into debt in the process.

- **I've got plenty of money left over at the end of a month.**

Maybe you're one of the blessed ones who have ample cash flow. Congratulations, but this is all the more reason to budget. Extra cash laying around in your account is so easy to let slip between your fingers. Maybe one day, your cash flow will be less and you'll wish you had a few of those "extra" dollars you let float away in earlier years.

As mentioned earlier, we have a serious responsibility to manage our wealth. The Bible has twice as many verses about money than faith and prayer combined! Other than the Kingdom of God, Jesus spoke about money more than any topic. Having a lot of wealth doesn't decrease that responsibility…it increases it. Can you have a larger amount of blow money each month for fun things? Sure. But if you don't have a plan, the blow money can blow a hole in your long-term plans.

Whatever your reason for not budgeting, rethink it. A great budget doesn't have to be pages and pages long (ours is only one page—front and back). And it doesn't have to take long. It can be a simple spreadsheet or even hand-written. The benefit isn't in the method used—it's in completing the task regardless of method.

If your budget improved the efficiency of your monthly spending by just 5%, what would your effective pay rate be for that one hour of work? Probably your most profitable hour of the month!

Whether you're wealthy or of limited income—we still have the duty and responsibility to God to manage the funds well. Simply paying your bills in full each month has absolutely no bearing on whether you are spending wisely and consistently with God's plan for you.

I find it interesting that I've never met someone who took budgeting seriously and later regretted it or felt it was a waste of time.

I always advise budgeting skeptics to make a good faith effort at budgeting for 90 to 120 days. If after that time you feel it's been unproductive, you can walk away knowing you tried. But I'm convinced that those who work diligently on creating a spending plan each month will quickly see the benefits and it will become one of the most productive and rewarding hours of your month. Are you willing to take that challenge?

Getting Started with Budgeting

Budgeting tools come in all shapes and sizes. It can be as simple as a legal pad or Excel spreadsheet. For those more tech savvy, low-cost (and free) software and apps also exist to help in the budget process. Regardless of which method you use, the basic process is the same.

For those who have never budgeted before, I always suggest they look forward by, first, looking back. As well as can be determined, look back to the expenditures in the previous month or two to see where your money went. Unless your bank balance grew, something happened to the money. Was it spent on expenses? If so, on what expenses was it spent and how much on each type? Was it sent to a savings or investment account? Was a portion of it donated?

There may be amounts you can't account for. A check was cashed or an ATM withdrawal was made and you don't remember what you did with the money. It's okay! Account for what you can—that's all anyone can ask of themselves.

With this information in hand, turn your attention to the upcoming month. In most instances, families have a reasonable idea of the income they are expecting the next month. Yes, there are instances of seasonal work or perhaps unpredictable commissions that make determining the amount of income difficult. But even in these situations a reasonable estimate of the next months expected income should be possible to determine.

Your next step will be to act like the coin sorter at a bank: allocate that estimated income into all the ways you plan to spend, save, invest, and give away those dollars. Every dollar should be accounted for! If you leave it unassigned it will surely be spent (more likely wasted) on some unknown purchase. Lost money like this is what slows down (or prevents entirely) you creating financial freedom and control.

When my family started creating a spending plan each month, we were shocked at how much we were spending in some categories with nothing to show for it. The budget allowed us to tell our money where to go instead of wondering where it went. Don't underestimate the value of going through the process.

A few budgeting tips to remember:

- Only budget one month at a time, and don't plan on doing it once and copying it over and over. Yes, many of the items will be the same month-to-month, but variables always arrive, whether it's a bonus at work, or an expense that only occurs quarterly or annually. Focus on just the next month.

- Your budget should total to zero. Your total monthly income should equal the total monthly "expenditures." This *doesn't* mean that you literally spend every dollar. It means that you account for every dollar by naming where it will go that month. Some of the dollars will, of course, go to the grocery store and the utility company. But some should (hopefully!) also be going to saving's accounts, your children's college fund, or be invested for retirement.

- For those who are married, your budget should be a collaborative process between a husband and wife, not a document prepared by one and forced on the other. It's fine for one to prepare the first draft of the budget, but both parties should have their voices heard and their priorities included in the spending plan.

- For those who are single, find an accountability partner! It is tough, especially in the first few months when it seems like a lot of work with limited benefit, to stick with creating a spending plan every month. Having someone to hold you accountable to do so will help tremendously. If possible, find someone going through the process on their own too, so you can hold each other accountable.

- Anticipate the budget process to not go well for several months. Budgeting is a skill and it takes time to learn. It also takes time for sporadic expenditures (that are easily forgotten) to reoccur and remind you of their existence.

- Once the budget is prepared, it should be treated as if it was prepared in pencil, not etched in stone. During the month, things will arise that weren't in the budget. When that happens, get back together with your spouse (if married) to adjust the budget as necessary. You're not in Congress, so if you need to spend more in one area, reduce another planned expenditure. Working on this together will not only solve the financial issue, but also strengthen your marriage in the process!

- The monthly planning process should continue, no matter what level of financial success you achieve. You never "graduate" from planning. The process will get easier and less time consuming as you gain experience.

Uses of Money to Be Budgeted

Besides budgeting for our expenses, what other uses of money should be included in our budgets each month?

There are, in fact, three specific uses of money that we all should keep in mind as we think about how to budget the funds that we have available. All three are important for different reasons and all three should be included in a healthy personal financial plan.

Use # 1 – Give it away

To many, this use will seem a bit strange. Winning at personal finance includes giving money away? Yes, it does.

As a Christian, the concept of giving money away is a central tenant of our faith. As mentioned in the chapter about tithing, God calls on us to cheerfully donate a portion of our income in recognition that it all comes from Him. Yes, I worked to earn the money, but He gave me the ability (through my knowledge and health) to make a living. To be clear, we're not saved by tithing and we don't live under the Old Testament law any longer, but it's a great practice to continue.

Besides living an obedient Christian walk, it's also well documented that giving to others benefits the giver as well as the recipient. Here are just a few ways:

- Increases happiness
- Reduces stress
- Reduces depression symptoms
- Improves the community in which we live
- Potential tax savings
- Reduces the power of money in our lives
- Increases gratitude

Use # 2 – Saving

Savings are required to meet three specific needs:

1. Emergency use

A significant reason for personal debt is the lack of an adequate emergency fund. Perhaps you were involved in a car accident. Maybe you incurred an unexpected medical emergency. Or you lost your job.

Situations like these often arise suddenly and without warning and the financial consequences can be devastating and long-lasting. The antidote to the financial stress that can easily come with situations like these is having an emergency fund.

Many financial advisers recommend we have three months to one year's worth of expenses set aside in a safe, FDIC-insured account. See Chapter 7 for more information about emergency funds.

2. Purchasing large-ticket items

Savings are also great for purchasing big-ticket items like cars, furniture, college tuition, and home improvements and repairs (ex. a new heat pump). There are two great benefits of using savings to pay for such items versus using promotional offers (like 90 days same as cash):

    a. When using cash, you don't get hit with unexpected interest charges from fine-print financing terms. The vast majority of promotional offers are *not* paid within the term of the interest free period. I know you meant to, but you get busy and forget a payment is due, which is exactly what the lender is counting on! Usually, these deals include terms that allow the lender to go back to the day of purchase to calculate the finance charge.

An example that I use in classes that I lead is for a mattress company promotion mailed to me a number of years ago. The ad offered seven-year financing at 0% interest as long as every payment was made on time. If a payment was late, interest would be charged on all of the payments from the date of purchase. I calculated some numbers on a hypothetical purchase and found that if you were late with the last (the 84th) payment, the accumulated interest that would be added to your balance was more than the original purchase price! So, you would owe more money than when you bought the mattress, and you have a seven-year-old mattress! Skip promotions like these. The terms are stacked against you.

b. When you use savings to purchase a big-ticket item, there is often (but not always) an opportunity to get a cash discount. We've personally received discounts on our insurance premiums, orthodontics, gym membership, and even newspaper subscriptions because we paid up front with cash. While, individually, the amount saved may not be huge, they can really add up over time! Larger savings are possible when using cash to pay for furniture or used cars.

3. Wealth building / retirement

The percentage of workers covered by a pension plan at work has been steadily declining. According to the Department of Labor, *"From 1980 through 2008, the proportion of private wage and salary workers participating in DB pension plans fell from 38 percent to 20 percent"* (Butrica, et al. 2009). Like it or not, today's American worker has to take more of the responsibility to save for their retirement than did earlier generations. Whether through a retirement plan (like a 401k) at work or on your own (in an IRA or taxable brokerage account), we need to save for retirement!

Eventually, either by choice or physical necessity, we will most likely have a period in our lives that won't include gainful employment. With the average Social Security benefit in 2019 amounting to only $1,461 per month, clearly, an additional source of income will be needed for many of us. Saving today for those future needs is the answer!

Use # 3 – Spending

I've grown accustomed to eating every day, having clothes on my back, and a roof over my head, so I'm in full agreement that this use is important to us all. The problem is that for many of us, it's the only way that we use money. In fact, many American families spend more than they make (thus the reason for the high debt situation in our nation)!

To get spending under control, the best method I've seen is to prepare a spending plan each month as described in this chapter. With practice, it gets easier and the benefits are immeasurable.

I am also a big advocate of limiting your lifestyle inflation. Simply put, as your income grows over time, limit your spending growth to only a portion of the income increase and allocate the rest for Uses #1 and #2. In my personal situation, this was a significant reason we've been able to grow our investment portfolio. It takes time, but it is time well spent (or said better, it is time well invested!).

A well-rounded personal financial plan should include all of these uses. It makes for a much better financial life and higher enjoyment of the resources you have available, both for today and the future!

Use Sinking Funds to Smooth the Budget

One of the challenges many budgeters face is how to handle the periodic payments that arise throughout the year. Scheduling the monthly rent or mortgage payment is easy, as are estimates for electricity (seasonally adjusted), telephones, and even gas and food. But what about the annual life insurance premiums? How about the semi-annual car insurance payments? Even events like Christmas can be a budgeting challenge. Do you budget your Christmas spending just in November and December (which can be tough if your budget is tight), or do you somehow spread the budgeting out all year? And how can you easily keep track of it all?

Enter the sinking fund. It's historically a term used in accounting to describe setting aside money for debt retirement or a large capital expenditure (think of a new roof or expensive piece of equipment that will need to be bought in the future). The company will simply set aside an amount (often fixed) each month for a set period of time, after which the funds needed to purchase the equipment or new roof will be readily available.

For a simple example, if the company needs a new $24,000 truck next year, they will set aside $2,000 per month for twelve months. Often, sinking funds are used for very large, multi-year projects. Imagine a large commercial building needing a $1,000,000 roof replacement every twenty-five years. It's a lot easier to set aside $3,333 per month for twenty-five years than to come up with $1,000,000 when the replacement is needed!

Let's do a little Q&A regarding sinking funds for our personal use:

Q. Why should we use a sinking fund approach for our personal finances?

Using a sinking fund is great not only for large-ticket items (like a car replacement), but also for irregular expenses throughout the year. We all face those large periodic expenses. Perhaps, in the past, we've stressed about how we'll come up with the amount due by the deadline.

The use of a sinking fund has eliminated the significant fluctuations in our monthly spending. It's much easier to set aside $100 every month than trying to come up with $1,200 at one time. Most of us don't have that much leeway in our monthly spending to cover a bill that large.

Q. What sort of expenses should be included in your sinking fund?

Personally, we use this principle for many of our irregular expenses:

- Annual automobile, homeowners, and umbrella premiums
- Personal Property Taxes
- Real Estate Taxes
- Christmas and other gifts
- Vacation
- Gym membership (paid annually for better pricing)
- School expenses, summer camps

Some expenses are lower if paid annually, so a sinking fund can actually save you money! For example, auto and home insurance are often less if paid in full at the beginning of the policy. Our gym offers three free months if we pay for a year in advance. Relatively, small savings like these really add up over the course of the year, so don't miss out on them!

You'll need to determine your own list. Scour your monthly spending plan for any items that will occur sometime during the year, but not on a monthly basis. If you pay your car insurance monthly, leave it in your budget. If you pay it annually as we do, include it in the sinking fund.

Of course, be reasonable. For small bills (for example, an annual $20 magazine subscription renewal), simply fund them with your regular cash flow during the month of renewal. Sinking funds should only be used for those expenses that can't be easily funded in one month's budget.

Q. How do we determine how much to add to the sinking fund each month?

Simply estimate the annual budgeted amount for each of the items you have selected to include in your sinking fund. Then total the individual estimates and divide by 12 to convert the annual total to a monthly amount. This freshly calculated monthly amount then appears on the spending plan (i.e., budget) each month.

An example might look something like this:

Item Description	Annual Amount
Automobile Insurance	$900.00
Christmas Gifts	750.00
Gym Membership	360.00
Life Insurance	255.00
Personal Property Taxes	1,035.00
Vacations	1,500.00
Total	$4,800.00
Monthly Amount (Total / 12)	$400.00

For this example, $400 would be added to your sinking fund each month and it would appear as a line item on your monthly budget, just like food and utilities.

Be sure to review these amounts each year as they will surely change. Some may be removed and others added.

Sinking Fund Case Study

This may sound complicated, but it really isn't! Let me illustrate with a case study:

Suppose your monthly income was $3,500 and your sinking fund contribution for the month was $400 (as calculated per the guidelines described earlier). Assuming (for simplicity's sake) you're opening your bank account with your first month's paycheck. Further, assume over the next three months, you'll have to pay your life insurance annual premium of $255 and your annual gym membership of $360, in addition to your regular monthly expenses. When you calculate your $400 sinking fund contribution amount, you include these two expenses.

Your check register might look something like this:

Our Checking Account

Date	Description	Amount	Balance ("A")
01/01/19	Pay check	3,500.00	3,500.00
01/01/19	Transfer to sinking fund	(400 00)	3,100.00
	(Other January activity)	(2,875 00)	225.00
02/01/19	Pay check	3,500.00	3,725.00
02/01/19	Transfer to sinking fund	(400 00)	3,325.00
	(Other February activity)	(2,975 00)	350.00
03/01/19	Pay check	3,500.00	3,850.00
03/01/19	Transfer to sinking fund	(400 00)	3,450.00
	(Other March activity)	(2,850 00)	600.00
04/01/19	Pay check	3,500.00	4,100.00
04/01/19	Transfer to sinking fund	(400 00)	3,700.00

Our Sinking Fund Balance

Date	Description	Amount	Balance ("B")	Account Total ("A" + "B")
			-	3,500.00
01/01/19	Transfer from checking	400.00	400 00	3,500.00
01/15/19	Pay life insurance	(255.00)	145 00	3,245.00
			145 00	370.00
02/01/19	Transfer from checking	400.00	545 00	3,870.00
			545 00	3,870.00
				895.00
03/01/19	Transfer from checking	400.00	545 00	4,395.00
03/22/19	Pay gym membership	(360.00)	945 00	4,395.00
			585 00	4,035.00
			585 00	1,185.00
04/01/19	Transfer from checking	400.00	585 00	4,685.00
			985 00	4,685.00

Each month, your pay check is deposited on the first. Immediately, $400 is transferred to your sinking fund. On 1/15/16 and 3/22/16, you paid the two bills being funded by the sinking fund.

Notice that those disbursements come from the sinking fund and not your checking account. Why? Because you've already set aside the money in the sinking fund! You no longer have to worry about how you'll come up with the $360 for the gym membership when it renews! You've planned ahead and have money resting comfortably awaiting the time when it's needed.

Q. Where do we keep the sinking fund balance until it's needed?

Some will choose to set up a dedicated savings account to transfer this amount to each month. Many banks will set up a free savings account and link it to your checking account, with easy online access. Ask your bank what options they offer.

Others, like ourselves, leave the money in our checking account, but we segregate it from the other spending money within the account. Allow me to explain: Notice in the case study above how the "Account Total" column to the far right didn't change when the sinking fund was funded. Since the money is still physically in the same account, it wouldn't change. When we complete our bank reconciliation each month, we'll use the "Account Total" column instead of the "Checking Account" balance.

As with all financial issues, you'll have to decide what works best for your situation.

Q. How do we handle the first year's sinking fund if bills come due before the money is available?

This sounds like a complicated question, but it's pretty straightforward. Let me ask it this way: Using the earlier example of a $400 per month sinking fund, how would you handle a $600 bill that is due in January if you only had $400 set aside at the time?

Suppose the actual payment schedule for the sinking fund items in our example were as follows:

Month	Amount Added	Bills Paid	Fund Balance
January	400.00	(255.00)	145.00
February	400.00		545.00
March	400.00	(360.00)	585.00
April	400.00	(1,035.00)	(50.00)
May	400.00		350.00
June	400.00		750.00
July	400.00		1,150.00
August	400.00	(1,500.00)	50.00
September	400.00		450.00
October	400.00	(900.00)	(50.00)
November	400.00		350.00
December	400.00	(750.00)	-
	4,800.00	(4,800.00)	

You will note the $400 being added each month and the bills being paid throughout the year. Both total $4,800 as expected. However, in both April and October, the sinking fund is negative! The total of the year-to-date bills due exceeds the amount contributed through that period of time. Of course, we can't have a negative sinking fund!

There are several possible solutions to this problem:

1. Make a one-time initial contribution to the sinking fund to cover the shortfall. In this example, it would require a $450 contribution in January. Doing so would keep April and October from going negative.

2. Bump up each of the contributions from January 1 to the first negative month by enough to cover the shortfall. In this example,

adding $12.50 to each of the first four month's contributions would eliminate the shortfall.

3. Cover the shortfall from that month's operating budget. For example, on your April budget, include $50 for Personal Property Taxes and only remove the available money from the sinking fund.

This is generally only an issue for the first year that you use a sinking fund. In later years, you should start the year with a "carry over" balance from the previous year to boost the balance high enough to cover large items early in the year. Continuing our example, here is Year 1 and Year 2 of the sinking fund balances (assuming you use option #3 above):

Month	Amount Added	Bills Paid	Fund Balance
January	400.00	(255.00)	145.00
February	400.00		545.00
March	400.00	(360.00)	585.00
April	400.00	(985.00)	-
May	400.00		400.00
June	400.00		800.00
July	400.00		1,200.00
August	400.00	(1,500.00)	100.00
September	400.00		500.00
October	400.00	(900.00)	-
November	400.00		400.00
December	400.00	(750.00)	50.00
Total for the year	4,800.00	(4,750.00)	
January	400.00	(255.00)	195.00
February	400.00		595.00
March	400.00	(360.00)	635.00
April	400.00	(1,035.00)	-
May	400.00		400.00
June	400.00		800.00
July	400.00		1,200.00
August	400.00	(1,500.00)	100.00
September	400.00		500.00
October	400.00	(900.00)	-
November	400.00		400.00
December	400.00	(750.00)	50.00
Total for the year	4,800.00	(4,800.00)	

Notice in April of Year 1 that I only withdrew the available amount of $985.00. The other $50 needed for the Personal Property Taxes will have to be added to the April budget. By handling it this way, you'll note the Year 1 December ending balance in the sinking fund is $50.00.

In April of Year 2, the full amount of the Personal Property Taxes is available in the sinking fund when they are due. Problem solved!

Closing Thoughts

Sinking funds are a great way to smooth out your spending and avoid some of the stress that can arise due to irregular due dates for some expenses. While your amounts will surely be different from those in our case study, you should be able to easily determine the amount you should use.

Keep in mind that this is not an exact science. Surely, your amounts won't come out as evenly as I've shown here (I know ours don't!). But with practice and determination, you, too, can develop a sinking fund strategy that works for your exact situation!

Scripture clearly calls for us to plan our financial lives in advance (Luke 14:28). Are you willing to follow this common sense request and maximize the value of every dollar God entrusts with you?

CHAPTER 5

WIPE OUT CONSUMER DEBT

*Owe no one anything except to love one another, for he who
loves another has fulfilled the law.*

ROMANS 13:8 (NKJV)

D ebt is a thief. It steals your ability to grow wealth. Every dollar you
send to creditors is one less dollar you could have invested. This
even applies to interest free loans. The cost of debt isn't just the interest you pay, it's also the growth in your wealth that you will never see
because some portion of your income is added to the profits of the lender
instead of yours.

I'm not aware of any scripture in the Bible that has anything positive
to say about debt. In fact, it speaks poorly of debt often and in clear language. Here are a few examples:

- Proverbs 22:7 (NKJV): *The rich rules over the poor, and the
  borrower is servant to the lender.*

   Christ set us free. Free from the penalty of sin. Free from the
   law. Free from legalism. Why chose to enslave ourselves to
   a lender?

- Galatians 5:1: *It is for freedom that Christ has set us free. Stand firm, then, and do not let yourselves be burdened again by a yoke of slavery.*

  Again, why choose to enslave ourselves to debt?

- Luke 14:28 (NKJV): *For which of you, intending to build a tower, does not sit down first and count the cost, whether he has enough to finish it.*

  This verse speaks not just to planning, but also to making sure you have enough resources to finish the job. Notice that it doesn't say to make sure your credit line is high enough to complete the work.

- Proverbs 17:18 (CEV[4]): *It's stupid to guarantee someone else's loan.*

  Don't cosign for someone else's debt. There's a reason the lender won't make the loan to the borrower without your signature: they don't think they'll get repaid, unless it's from you. If you're in the financial position to do so, give them a gift to help them, but don't guaranty their obligations!

The best way to handle consumer debt is to simply not borrow money (except for, perhaps, purchasing a home which will be covered in an upcoming chapter). Never borrowing means never having to dig out of a debt hole. Since borrowing should be off limits, an adequate emergency fund[5] is important to replace what would be borrowed in a time of sudden need.

But I'm already in debt!

If you already have consumer debt, don't beat yourself up about it! We've all made mistakes with money, sometimes huge mistakes. What matters now is what you are going to do about it. Don't look back with

---

[4] Contemporary English Version. I normally don't use this version of the Bible, but the way they worded this verse was too good to not use!

[5] Emergency funds are discussed in more detail in Chapter 7.

regret; look forward with hope and a commitment to get rid of your debt. Eliminate that thief from your life as quickly as possible. Remove the chains of debt and instead enjoy the fruits of your labor as God intended.

How to get rid of debt?

Personal finance is much more about the "personal" than the "finance," as many (myself included) have often noted. Said a different way: Understanding how we think, what our goals and objectives are, what we fear, and what motivates us is vital to our financial success. This is true not because it's always mathematically the absolute right solution, but because it recognizes who we are and how we think.

Such is the case with paying off your consumer debt. Different theories are easy to find, but which one will really help you most effectively pay off your debts? Which will help you stay motivated to complete a process that may take years depending on your income, expenses, and debt load?

Regardless of which debt payment strategy you use, let's set some guidelines:

- First, you should be operating your finances with a monthly spending plan. See Chapter 4 to learn how to do this properly. This will maximize the efficiency of each dollar of income you have available. No dollar is wasted or lost to frivolous spending.
- Second, make a complete list of your non-mortgage debts. List every credit card, car loan, personal loan, payday loan, and student loan you have. It may be painful to see, but ignoring it won't make it go away and doing so will make it much more painful in the long run.
- Third, make sure you're making the minimum payment on each debt and that they are included on your spending plan mentioned above. Falling behind on one loan to get ahead on another doesn't make sense. Should it happen, many loan agreements allow the

lender to dramatically increase your interest rate, even if you weren't late on their payment!

- Next, do you have additional money available each month (above the minimum payments) to go toward paying off debt? If you don't, it doesn't matter which order you're paying the debts as you're only making the minimum payments. You will need to either increase your income or decrease your expenses. Even better, do both!

So, let's assume you've listed your debts and have some available cash flow each month (after the minimum payments) to put toward paying them off faster than scheduled. Here is where the differing opinions arise. When it comes to debt elimination strategies, a quick search on the Internet will provide many opinions about how to do it most effectively.

Advisers will advocate:

- Paying the highest interest rate balances first
- Focusing on the smallest balances first
- Paying the most "painful" ones first (for example, owing the IRS or a family member you have to see at Thanksgiving!)
- Eliminating "secured" debt first (since a failure to repay them could cause you to lose your car, for example), then pay off the unsecured debtors.
- Combinations of these strategies, creating an even more complicated repayment strategy.

They'll be given fancy names like the *"debt snowball,"* the *"debt avalanche,"* and the *"debt tsunami"* (these are all actual names of payment strategies). Each one seems to be trying to outdo the previous.

It's certainly true that arguments can be made for any of these (and the many other) strategies out there, but which is best? Can we keep this simple—and effective—or do we need to outthink ourselves? And where do nonmonetary issues, like motivation, come in?

Usually,[6] my recommendation is to list the debts smallest to largest and pay them off in that order. When the smallest debt is paid completely, take the full amount you were paying on that debt and apply it to the next debt on the list. This is in addition to the minimum payment you're making on that next debt.

Yes, this does mean to ignore the interest rates being charged. However, in many cases, the interest rate difference is not significant enough to ignore what works better in the real world—when emotions and motivations are taken into account.

Let's look at an example to see my point:

In our hypothetical example, imagine having the following debts:

	Balance	**Interest Rate**	**Minimum Payment**
Loan 1	12,000.00	8%	455.00
Loan 2	6,000.00	6%	350.00
Loan 3	5,500.00	5%	125.00
Loan 4	2,500.00	2%	70.00
	———		———
	26,000.00		1,000.00

Maybe they're student loans, car loans, or credit cards. The source doesn't matter. The minimum payments total $1,000, and assume further that through the use of a great spending plan we have **an extra $500 per month** to put toward paying them off early.

---

[6] Generally, this will be my advice to coaching clients, however there are always exceptions. For example, if a client had a $10,000 / 0% auto loan and an $11,000 / 21% credit card, clearly the credit card should be paid first, even though its balance is slightly larger. Common sense should always be used when determining how to proceed. A case like this is exceptionally rare, though.

If you pay them using *"smallest to largest balance,"* here is the result:

Debt Snowball
Smallest to Largest Balance

	Balance	Interest Rate	Minimum Payment	Paid Off Month	Interest Paid
Loan 1	2,500.00	2%	70.00	5.00	11.39
Loan 2	5,500.00	5%	125.00	12.00	186.31
Loan 3	6,000.00	6%	350.00	14.00	266.55
Loan 4	12,000.00	8%	455.00	19.00	1,000.18
	26,000.00		1,000.00		1,464.43

If you pay them using *"highest to lowest interest rate,"* here is the result:

Debt Snowball
Highest to Lowest Interest Rate

	Balance	Interest Rate	Minimum Payment	Paid Off Month	Interest Paid
Loan 1	12,000.00	8%	455.00	14.00	574.75
Loan 2	6,000.00	6%	350.00	15.00	274.33
Loan 3	5,500.00	5%	125.00	18.00	320.51
Loan 4	2,500.00	2%	70.00	19.00	181.56
	26,000.00		1,000.00		1,351.15

In both cases, it took nineteen months to pay off all of the balances. The interest savings you would realize if you paid the highest rate first would be only $113.28! This works out to less than $6 for each of the nineteen months.

Here is the key for me: Using the smallest balance first method, the first victory (i.e., paying off the first item) occurred in *only five months*.

Think how great it would feel to get that first one out of your life. Then the second is paid off in only seven more months and the third is gone only two months after that! I see those victories as being huge in maintaining your motivation to keep going.

It would take fourteen months to pay off the first debt using the highest interest rate first method. If you can stay motivated that long without paying one off, feel free to do so and save the $6 per month. But I've found that most people need the quick victories to keep going (Remember, it's more "personal" than "finance"!). Research backs up this theory. In August 2015, a study published in the *Journal of Marketing Research* found that paying off the smallest balance first led to more debt being paid off overall.

> *"Winning what are known as 'small victories' by paying off small debts first can give consumers a real boost in eventually paying off all their debts,"* write the authors of the study, Alexander L. Brown (Texas A&M University) and Joanna N. Lahey (Texas A&M University). *"The reason is that meeting a small goal provides the motivation to then meet a larger goal"* (Journal of Marketing Research 2015).

Obviously, the most important factor in paying off your debts is to pay as much as possible toward them, regardless of the order you pay them off. But if you have funds available to make extra payments, use them in a way to keep you motivated to finish the task. For most of us, it will be paying the smallest balance first.

What to do if you're already behind on debt payments?

Perhaps you find yourself already behind on the payments for your debts. I know it can be stressful, but through diligence and trust in God to provide, there is a pathway to getting caught up and clearing the debts. Here's what I recommend:

- **Make sure you have $1,000 in emergency savings collected first.** No matter how well you plan your expenses, something unexpected seems to pop up periodically and it's good to be financially prepared.
- If the creditors are not calling right now, the debt may have been charged off. I would not contact them at this time. Instead, I'd recommend you **begin to accumulate "*debt settlement*" money**. Set aside as much as your monthly budget allows. Keep your spending as low as possible to quickly accumulate extra cash.
- **List your past due debt in smallest-to-largest balance order.** Once you have about 50% of the smallest debt saved in cash (*not* counting your $1,000 emergency fund), contact the first collection company (the one with the lowest balance owed). Offer them 50% of the amount owed to settle the debt *in full*. They may well take the offer as they are not expecting to collect anything at this point. Most likely, they bought the past due debt for pennies on the dollar from another creditor, so a 50% settlement deal will result in a profit for them.
- **If they refuse, say, "Okay, I'll move on to another creditor."** They may quickly change their mind! If they don't, continue saving each month until you get to 50% of the next largest debt. Then try the 50% settlement offer with the second creditor.
- Once you've made your way through the list, **go back to the beginning and make the same offer to any that didn't accept it the first time** (again, after you've saved up enough cash to immediately send the agreed upon payment). They may be more willing to accept it the second time around.

Over time, settling these accounts will help your credit score and remove the charge-off from your file. **Just remember to "wake up" only one creditor at a time!** Make a deal with them (if possible) and then move to the next creditor.

Should a creditor sue you in court to collect past due balances, you may need to seek bankruptcy protection to prevent excessive garnishment of your wages. *Should you find yourself in this situation, please contact a local attorney familiar with the bankruptcy and collection laws in your area to assist you in this process.*

If you reach an agreement with a creditor and are going to send payment, here are some important things to remember:

- Only send payment after you have received confirmation **IN WRITING** that the payment will settle the account **IN FULL**. An emailed confirmation is fine. **GET IT IN WRITING BEFORE SENDING PAYMENT.**
- **Do not allow them electronic access to your account**—ever. They may take more than the agreed upon amount!
- Go to your bank and **get a cashier's check and mail it via USPS Priority Mail**. This will provide you a tracking number to prove they received it. The cashier's check will keep them from knowing your personal checking account number. It will cost a few bucks in postage (and possibly a fee for the cashier's check) but it is well worth it.
- **Keep a file with their written confirmation of settlement, a copy of the cashier's check, and a print out of the delivery confirmation FOREVER.** They may pop back up years from now saying you owe them more money. If that happens, send them copies of the written confirmation, cashier's check and delivery confirmation.

Stick to these steps and eventually, you'll be debt free and your credit score will begin to improve over time. Don't quit or get discouraged. Most likely, the debts accumulated over time and it will take some time to clear them up. But it can be done!

Closing Thoughts

During the real estate crash in the late 2000s, a scheme called "*strategic default*" came into existence. Due to the sudden drop in home values, many borrowers found themselves owing more on a home than it was worth. Instead of continuing to make payments—as they promised in the loan documents—they simply turned in the keys and walked away. These borrowers had the financial resources to make the payment, they simply chose not to because the market value of their home dropped. **Note: I am not speaking here of borrowers who could not make their payments due to job loss, health issues, etc.**

Scripture is clear about honoring our promises to repay. Psalm 37:21 begins, "*The wicked borrow and do not repay.*" Romans 13:7 (ESV) counsels us to "*Pay to all what is owed to them.*" Choosing to walk away from your debts because you made a bad home purchase is wrong. You promised to repay borrowed money. Nothing in the loan documents removes this obligation simply because the housing market drops. Further, I've never heard of a borrower paying extra to the lender when the housing market is booming so that they, too, can share in unexpected growth. We can't keep the boom year profits for ourselves but then make the bank cover the losses in the down years. Honor your obligations as God would have you to do.

God never intended us to be slaves to anyone. We are spiritually free, but often remain a slave to those to whom we owe money. Shake lose the debt shackles through commitment to a debt free plan. Financial freedom is waiting.

Are you willing to be set free financially?

CHAPTER 6

ACCUMULATE DIVERSIFIED WEALTH OVER TIME

Invest in seven ventures, yes, in eight; you do not know what disaster may come upon the land.

ECCLESIASTES 11:2

S aving and building wealth for use in the future is encouraged in the Scripture. Even the lowly ant is praised in Proverbs 6 for using a portion of today's harvest for future needs. Likewise, we are to use some of the current resources God has provided to save and invest for our future needs. Proverbs 21:20 (NKJV) states, "There is desirable treasure, and oil in the dwelling of the wise, but a foolish man squanders it." The wise have saved a portion of his gain for future use, while it's deemed foolish to use all that you have received. Today, we most likely will not have oil stored in our homes. However, we may well have stocks, bonds, or mutual funds as an instrument in which to store wealth. This wealth is not just for our needs, but as instructed in Ephesian 4:28 (NKJV), it is so we will "have something to give him who has need."

Satan looks for any opportunity to turn God's Word and wisdom into destructive behavior. Growing wealth is no exception. If we are saving, investing, and growing our wealth out of fear or greed, God's instruction is being perverted. Being motivated by fear indicates a lack of trust in God to provide for our needs. Growing wealth out of greed turns our attention away from God as we credit ourselves and our shrewd investing for our gain. Both are clearly sinful and not what God intends for us. It has been said that money magnifies our heart. If we are deeply committed to God and His vision for our lives, wealth gives us additional opportunities to serve Him. However, if our hearts are inward looking, placing our wants and desires above all else, money is the means by which our selfish desires manifest themselves. We then have the ability to live outwardly the selfish thoughts of our inner selves. Never substitute wealth for God's place as our provider, protector, and defender. "Do not lay up for yourselves treasures on earth, where moth and rust destroy and where thieves break in and steal" (Matthew 6:19 NKJV).

Having established a spending plan and successfully dealt with non -mortgage debt (by eliminating it as quickly as possible), we're financially positioned to begin building wealth. Our savings goal, in general, is to dedicate 15% of our gross income toward building wealth for retirement. If you start early in your career, you may be able to save a slightly lower percentage (although I'd still recommend 15% as future earnings are unknowable today). If you delay until late in your working years, savings rates of 25%, 30%, or more may be required to fund retirement in the few remaining years of your career. If you haven't been diligent about saving through your career, don't be discouraged! Remember, "And my God shall supply all your need according to His riches in glory by Christ Jesus" (Philippians 4:19 NKJV). Yes, the best day to start saving for retirement was twenty years ago. The next best day is today, so let's get started.

Investing 101 – How to Invest Wisely

Through my time spent working with individuals and small business owners, I've had the opportunity to counsel and coach them on numerous topics. One topic over which many people struggle is the management of their investments. Regardless of the size of their portfolio, they struggle with devising a proper investment policy, one they feel comfortable following regardless how the market performs. Often, even a well-thought-out plan will be spontaneously changed by human emotions during periods of market turmoil. This lack of commitment to a plan leads to a couple of common mistakes:

- *A "mish-mash" of investments*. Often, the investor will chase returns by buying the hot investment from last year. Or they will purchase several investments of the same type because they "feel" they will outperform the market. This "feeling" could be based on something they read on the Internet, or a hot stock tip supplied by a friend. Eventually, the poorly constructed portfolio will fail to perform as expected and the investor will bail out, possibly after taking significant losses. Then, when the market inevitably rebounds, they're not in a position to recover those losses.

- *Do nothing*. The other reaction is the exact opposite. The lack of a plan breeds fear and stagnation. Unsure of who to trust, the investor opts for leaving their investments sitting in cash or certificates of deposit. With today's low interest rates, the real return on their money is below zero as inflation will erode the purchasing power of their savings. Eventually, some of the "do nothing" investors will finally work up the nerve to enter the investing market, but usually only after the market has risen substantially. Often, they will come in at or near a market peak— missing out on the gains captured during the bull market, only to suffer outsized losses when the market again declines. Then, of course, they will sell, locking in those losses and vowing to never invest again (at least until there has been another sustained market increase that they missed…again).

Both of these situations can be avoided by developing a rational, well-thought-out plan to manage your investments, preferably in advance of actually investing. Fortunately, it's not as difficult as many financial professionals would lead you to believe. The vast majority of investors are fully capable of managing their investments, if they take the time to educate themselves and devise an investing plan. Should you feel the need to seek professional help, there are many ethical financial advisors, truly interested in your financial success. Unfortunately, the industry is also filled with those selling high commission products that benefit their family more than yours. Make sure any advisor you use is a "fiduciary," who must put your interest above their own. For more suggestions about selecting an advisor, please review the recommendations in frequently asked questions section at the end of this chapter.

Through this chapter I hope to inspire you to take control of your investments, understand your options, and develop and implement a reasonable plan to capture market returns. Our goal shouldn't be to "beat" the market as this usually leads to taking more risk than is acceptable. Be sure you have an understanding of each concept discussed, otherwise you'll not stick to your plan during difficult investment cycles.

The decisions regarding your investments are yours. Opting not to decide is a decision in itself, and one that will decrease the time a well-planned portfolio has to grow. The goal of this chapter is to help you make sound decisions in a logical manner that comply with scriptural guidelines.

Pre-Investing Decisions

Surprisingly enough, successful investing doesn't begin with research on the hottest stocks or industries. Instead, it's important to first examine yourself before attempting to make decisions regarding your investing. To repeat an earlier principle, "personal finance" is much more *personal* than *finance*. Trying to copy an investment strategy that works well for a friend or family member will probably not work equally well for you.

Factors such as age, work status, retirement goals, and risk tolerance differ from person to person, and the variances in these factors will impact what a "successful" investing strategy may look like for an individual.

Let's explore a few questions and issues that should be understood before devising your own investment strategy:

- ***Should I even be investing?***

For purposes of this chapter, let's define *saving* vs. *investing*. All of us need to have savings set aside for unforeseen circumstances. This savings should be in a safe account, such as an FDIC insured bank savings or money market account. To increase the interest slightly, perhaps three months of the savings could be put into a certificate of deposit (CD). Be sure to compare interest rates to make sure it makes sense to commit the funds to the CD. As budgeting and debt guru Dave Ramsey advocates, consider this type of savings as *insurance* for bad times, not something on which you're trying to earn a return. Instead, it is to have increased financial security against unforeseen expenses or negative events, such as the loss of a job. Unfortunately, a negative event will happen to us all at some point…the savings account is there to cushion the financial blow. Borrowing money, or selling investments prematurely, to deal with the situation will only compound the financial problems. Chapter 7 will cover emergency funds in greater detail.

Investing, on the other hand, is for long-term growth, not short-term security. It is only after setting aside a reasonable amount of "emergency money" should you approach the subject of investing.

Additionally, strong consideration should be given to paying off *non-mortgage* debt prior to beginning a sustained investing program. Often, the best return on your money is eliminating debt and the interest payments that come along with it. This will also free up additional funds each month that can be added to your monthly investing.

Finally, determine how long you'll have until you'll need the resources that you're considering investing. History has shown markets can go through *multiyear* underperforming periods, and being forced to sell an investment because the funds are needed elsewhere simply serves to lock in your losses and costs you the opportunity to recoup your losses when the inevitable market rebound occurs. However, history has also shown that being able to leave assets invested for ten or more years significantly increases the probability of long-term gains. A recent study showed that the *worst* average annual performance for any ten-year term was a loss of 2.07%. Further, there were *no* twenty- or thirty-year investment terms (since 1871) that resulted in an average annual loss.[7] Keep in mind your time frame when deciding how to allocate your investments (as discussed later). If you know you'll need funds in five years or less (for example, for college expenses), the funds should *not* be invested in the stock market or similar volatile assets.

- ### *What are the common types of investment?*

For the average investor today, the most logical places to invest are in stocks and bonds. They offer a great diversification of risk, and can be purchased (if done correctly) at a very low cost. This has not always been the case, but we are blessed to live in an era when the competition in the marketplace has significantly reduced the costs to invest.

Stocks are shares of ***ownership*** in a company. Publicly traded companies issue millions of shares so your ownership will only be a fraction of a percent. But this small ownership allows you to realize some of the gains in the value of their shares over time. You should do well if the company succeeds, or potentially lose your investment if the company goes bankrupt. Within the stock (also known as equity) markets are both large and small companies, domestic and international companies, growth companies, and value[8] stocks. In summary, stocks offer a bigger upside potential…but also a bigger downside potential.

---

[7] Source: Wisdom Tree Asset Management, as published in Barron's, December 9, 2013.

[8] Value stocks are those "that tend to trade at a lower price relative to its fundamentals (i.e. dividends, earnings, sales, etc.) and thus considered undervalued" (Smith 2019).

Bonds, on the other hand, represent **debt** *of the issuer*. The bond issuer promises to repay to the bondholders a fixed amount on a certain date with periodic, scheduled interest payments along the way. Should the issuer go bankrupt (or for some reason be unable to meet their obligations), you could potentially lose all or a portion of your investment. Although rare for highly rated bonds, it can happen.

For corporate bonds, the bondholders must be paid *before* shareholders, so you have less risk than if you owned the stock of the exact same company. In summary, bonds are less risky, which will also limit their potential returns.

Here's an important point to remember: Risk *always* parallels the potential returns. The higher the risk, the higher the potential returns (which is the only reason to take on the added risk). The higher the potential returns of an investment, the higher risk will be.

In addition to corporate bonds, investors have the option of investing in municipal bonds, which are bonds issued by states and municipalities. Municipal bonds have historically paid lower rates of interest; however, they are not subject to federal income tax (and sometimes they are exempt from state income taxes as well). Therefore, especially for high income investors, the after-tax return can be higher for municipal bonds vs. bonds which interest is taxable income.

One final point on bonds and risk. Changes in interest rates will affect the market value of a bond. The longer the remaining term of a bond, the more sensitivity (up or down) it will have to interest rate changes. Here's why: Remember, bonds typically pay a fixed rate of interest. Imagine owning a bond paying the current market rate of interest, for example 3%, and then the market rate of interest *increases* to 4%. What happens to the value of your bond? Even though nothing about the specific terms of your bond has changed, the fact that your bond now pays *below* what a potential buyer could get elsewhere means that your bond is worth less to him or her. If you were buying a bond, wouldn't a bond that pays 4% be worth more to you than one that only pays 3%? The good news is that the opposite is also true. If market interest rates fall, the bonds you already own become more valuable for the same reason.

The longer the time until your bond matures, the more significant the change in value will be, as the bond will have longer to pay a higher (or lower) rate of interest. Therefore, investors will experience more volatility (up and down) with a *long-term* bond fund than a *short-term* fund.

- ### *How much should you have in stock funds vs. bond funds?*

Now that we have a basic understanding of stocks vs. bonds, how much do we allocate to each broad class? Based on our previous discussion, the more one allocates to stocks the higher the potential return but also the higher the potential loss. Likewise, a higher allocation to bonds may offer less risk but will also produce less of a return. Traditional asset allocation theory calls for a higher stock allocation when the investor is young, with ever increasing bond allocations as the investor ages. When we are younger, we can afford to take more risk as we'll have many more years to make up for loss in value from a market correction. Further, young investors typically have smaller investment accounts, so the losses incurred tend to be smaller (in dollars). Finally, young investors are usually making regular monthly contributions (through, for example, a 401k plan), and those periodic investments will purchase more shares at the lower prices prevalent after a market correction.

As we age, we'll have less time to make up for a major correction, therefore, we should consider lowering the stock allocation to lessen the risk. Bonds should be viewed as a tool to lessen the risk of a portfolio. They are not in the portfolio for growth; they are included to cushion the blow from a dramatic stock market drop in value. Remember: Stocks are for growth; bonds are for safety.

The following chart shows the *best*, *worst*, and *average* returns for various stock and bond allocations from 1926 to 2012 (Vanguard 2014).

Allocation		Average	Best	Worst
Stocks	Bonds	Return	Return	Return
100%	0%	10.00%	54.20%	-43.10%
90%	10%	9.70%	49.80%	-39.00%
80%	20%	9.40%	45.40%	-34.90%
70%	30%	9.10%	41.10%	-30.70%
60%	40%	8.70%	36.70%	-26.60%
50%	50%	8.30%	32.30%	-22.50%
40%	60%	7.80%	27.90%	-18.40%
30%	70%	7.30%	28.40%	-14.20%
20%	80%	6.70%	29.80%	-10.10%
10%	90%	6.20%	31.20%	-8.20%
0%	100%	5.50%	32.60%	-8.10%

As you can see, as the allocation to stocks increases, both the *best* and the *average* returns improve. However, the *worst* returns also increase. The key is to find the allocation with the highest percentage allocated to stocks that you feel comfortable sticking with during the bad periods. For example, assume you select a 90% stock allocation. Historical returns from 1926 to 2012 have shown that such an allocation would have yielded a *"worst"* year result of a 39% decrease in value. If suffering such a loss would lead you to sell your investments, your stock allocation is too high. *Don't minimize the real emotional trauma such a loss brings to many investors*. Take seriously the responsibility to consider how large a loss you can suffer and not sell your investments. Many investors take this issue too lightly and then sell when the worst case happens (and eventually, it probably will). Think about real-life scenarios. For example, if your $10,000 investment portfolio went to $6,100 in one year, what would you do? Buy more because stocks were "on sale"? Or sell your remaining investments to "hold on to what's left"? Perhaps, at that level of investment, you'd ride it out. Now, suppose it was a $1,000,000 portfolio that is now worth $610,000—a $390,000 loss in value. Would your answer be the same?

There are many excellent online risk assessment calculators that are free to use. Vanguard's questionnaire,[9] for example, takes only a few minutes to complete and can shed some light on your personal risk tolerance. I'd recommend using several of these tools and average the results to begin to hone in on your tolerance for risk. Additional factors to consider about risk follow in Chapter 7.

In late 2013, a year during which the stock market gained significantly, a friend lamented that he sold his stock investments in 2007 and 2008 following a dramatic drop in the market. Clearly, he had underestimated his risk tolerance, and therefore sold his investments instead of holding steady (or even better, buying more shares while prices were down). If his allocation had been more to his internal risk tolerance, all of the losses he suffered in 2007 and 2008 would have been recouped by 2013. Instead, the losses were locked in and he missed out on a great market recovery.

There is no "wrong" answer when it comes to an allocation between stocks and bonds. But it is important to not simply copy someone else's plan. Their level of risk tolerance could be (and probably would be) different from yours. Choose the one that works for you.

A general guideline that many investors follow is to hold their age in bonds. So, for example, a forty-year-old investor would hold 40% in bonds and 60% in stocks. However, this is only a general rule that many investors disagree with, so be sure to decide this on your own. It's a fair place to start, but your individual tolerance for risk can substantially change this guideline.

I believe every investor should hold at least some bonds and some stock funds. Having at least some stock funds allows an investor the opportunity to participate in a rising market while limiting their exposure to a large decrease from a bear market. Holding at least some bond funds will provide a pool of money to move into stocks when there is a market correction.

- ***What type of stock and bond funds should I buy?***

History has shown that the performance of various investing sectors changes each year. The following chart ranks the various market segments performance results from 1993 to 2012.

---

[9] Vanguard's risk questionnaire can be found at https://personal.vanguard.com/us/FundsInvQuestionnaire.

Historical Returns By Asset Class

Rank (Best → Worst)	1993	1994	1995	1996	1997	1998	1999	2000	2001	2002	2003	2004	2005	2006	2007	2008	2009	2010	2011	2012
Best Performer	EM	INT	500 GR	500 GR	500 GR	500 GR	EM	SML VL	SML VL	BOND	EM	EM	EM	EM	EM	BOND	EM	SML GR	BOND	EM
	INT	500 GR	500	500	500	500	SML GR	BOND	BOND	EM	SML GR	SML VL	INT	INT	INT	SML VL	SML GR	SML	500 GR	SML VL
	SML VL	500	500 VA	500 VA	SML VL	INT	500 GR	500 VA	SML	SML VL	SML	INT	500 VA	SML VL	500 GR	SML	INT	SML VL	500	500 VA
	SML	500 VA	SML GR	SML VL	500 VA	500 VA	INT	SML	EM	INT	SML VL	SML	500	500 VA	SML GR	500 GR	500 GR	EM	500 VA	INT
	500 VA	SML VL	SML	SML	SML	BOND	SML	500	SML GR	SML	INT	500 VA	SML VL	SML	BOND	500	SML	500 VA	SML GR	SML
	SML GR	SML	SML VL	SML GR	SML GR	SML GR	500	INT	500 VA	500 VA	500	SML GR	SML	500	500	SML GR	500	500 GR	SML	500
	500	SML GR	BOND	INT	BOND	SML	500 VA	500 GR	500	500	500 GR	500	500 GR	SML GR	500 VA	500 VA	500 VA	INT	SML VL	500 GR
	BOND	BOND	INT	EM	INT	SML VL	BOND	SML GR	500 GR	500 GR	BOND	500 GR	SML GR	500 GR	SML	INT	SML VL	BOND	INT	SML GR
Worst Performer	500 GR	EM	EM	BOND	EM	EM	SML VL	EM	INT	SML GR	500 VA	BOND	BOND	BOND	SML VL	EM	BOND	500	EM	BOND

LEGEND

BOND	Bond Fund (Aggregate)
EM	Emerging Markets
INT	International
SML	Small Cap
SML GR	Small Cap Growth
SML VL	Small Cap Value
500	S&P 500
500 GR	S&P 500 Growth
500 VA	S&P 500 Value

As you'll note, there is no discernable pattern as to which segment performed the best in any given year. Therefore, attempting to predict which segment will perform best in the future is impossible. There may be reasons to expect particular segments to do well or to do poorly, but to consistently and accurately predict which segment will do so is unrealistic. Should you select the incorrect market segment for a particular year, your portfolio can suffer a significant loss based on that segment's performance. *Remember, we're trying to match the markets performance, not figure out a way to "beat the market." Doing so requires investors to take unnecessary risks.*

The safest way to manage this risk is through diversification. When you diversify across the market segments, you have some exposure to *all* the areas. If you can't predict which one or two will perform well over the upcoming year, own them all! Fortunately, you can do so very easily with minimal costs, as will be discussed later.

History has shown that a low-cost, diversified portfolio outperforms those trying to predict the next "hot" sector. Sometimes they may be right and will outperform the market in a particular year, but predicting in advance which one it will be next year is impossible to do routinely.

- ### *What types of accounts can hold my investments?*

There are multiple types of accounts in which an investor can hold their investments. As a general rule, the most significant difference between the types of accounts is the way in which they're taxed. Minimizing taxes is important. Having to reduce your portfolio in order to pay a tax bill will decrease the long-term growth of the portfolio.

The most common type of account investors will use to hold their securities is through a tax-deferred or tax-free structure. *Traditional* IRAs and 401k plans allow participants to save money using *pre-tax* earnings and the growth of the investments remain untaxed until withdrawn from the account. *Roth* IRAs and 401k plans are funded with *after-tax* money but, under most circumstances, distributions from them will *not* be taxed. There are limitations on who, and how much, can be added annually to an IRA or 401k. *Please note that these are general rules and you should consult a tax advisor for your own particular situation.*

An additional common account type would be an *individual* or *taxable* account. In this type of account, the investments are purchased with *after-tax* dollars and, unlike an IRA, any activity in the account during the year would be taxed in that current year.

Some types of mutual funds produce high distributions (interest or dividends) each year. Therefore, consideration should be given for which investments are placed in which type of an account. For example, real estate investment trusts (REIT)[10] traditionally distribute high dividends each year. Further, these dividends are traditionally taxed at the investor's highest marginal tax rate. Therefore, should an investor decide to own REITs, they should place them in a tax preferred account, such as an IRA or 401k plan. Conversely, municipal bonds should be held in a taxable account as they earn interest free of federal income tax liability. One would lose the benefit of the tax-free status of the municipal bond if it was held in a tax-preferred account.

In my experience, many investors have limited funds in taxable accounts, primarily because they've chosen to invest through their employer's 401k plan. However, having funds in a taxable account increases the withdrawal options available to an investor when that time arrives. While taxes become an issue to be managed when dealing with taxable accounts, investors shouldn't hesitate to use them if they've exhausted their tax-preferred options.

- *Why is inflation so dangerous?*

It's very tempting for investors to want to limit the volatility in their portfolio by increasing the level of bonds held. While this historically would have made the portfolio less risky, it also makes the portfolio more susceptible to the dangers of inflation. The long-term impact of inflation on the value of a portfolio is undeniable. While annual inflation increases

---

[10] REITs invest in and own properties (thus responsible for the equity or value of their real estate assets). Their revenues come primarily from their properties' rents (Chen 2019).

can seem minor, the cumulative effect erodes the purchasing power of the money you save. For example, a $100 item today will increase to over $181 in thirty years at only a 2% annual inflation rate. With our extended life expectancies (compared to earlier generations), a thirty-plus-year retirement span is reasonable to assume for a sixty-five-year-old retiree.

One of the limitations of typical bond investments is that they historically offer lower returns and thus little return above inflation. The way to combat this is with an increase in the equity portion of the portfolio allocation. Don't use riskier bonds, like junk bonds, to increase your return. Bonds of this type are called "junk" for a reason. If you're comfortable taking risk (which you would need to be to consider lower-rated bonds like this), you're better served by investing more into the stock market that has provided higher long-term performance. Recall the earlier principle: bonds are for safety, not for growth. "Junk" bonds are not safe.

In determining your asset allocation, be careful to not be too conservative in order to avoid risk. Over time, inflation will erode your portfolio's value.

- ### *What are some important investing terms?*

Before moving on to the principles of solid investing, there are a few investing terms to define since you'll likely be exposed to them during your research for investments.

Often, potential investors can be intimidated by the terminology used in investing literature. However, the beginning investor shouldn't allow themselves to be deterred from investing. Understanding the basic terminology can be easily grasped by new investors.

Don't allow yourself to sit on the sidelines of investing because you don't understand every investing term. Successful investing is about having a reasonable, well-thought-out plan and sticking to it.

Let's examine a few of the most important terms you may run across as you invest:

- We'll begin by defining an *"actively managed mutual fund"* and an *"index mutual fund,"* as both are readily available for investors.

   Actively managed funds "rely on analytical research, forecasts, and their own judgment and experience in making investment decisions on what securities to buy, hold, and sell. The opposite of active management is called passive management, better known as 'indexing'" (Chen, Active Management 2018). The cost of researching and trading stocks is an expense of the mutual fund and typically result in higher fees paid by the funds investors (i.e. you!).

   An index mutual fund has "a portfolio constructed to match or track the components of a market index, such as the Standard & Poor's 500 Index (S&P 500)" (Chen, Index Fund 2019). Since the managers are merely tracking a predefined list of stocks, like the S&P 500, it is much less costly, spreads the risk among many companies, and has very little trading (buying and selling the company stock owned by the fund).

   The choice between these two options will be discussed in the "Investing Empowerment Principles" section later in the chapter.

- The next term to understand is *standard deviation*. Standard deviation, according to Investopedia.com, is "a statistical measurement that sheds light on historical volatility" (Hargrave 2019). Put simply, it measures how varied the returns on an investment have been. So, for example, a large stable blue-chip company would have a low standard deviation—the annual variations tend to be less pronounced. Blue-chip companies would include Coca-Cola, Johnson & Johnson, McDonalds, and Walmart. On the other hand, a start-up Internet company would traditionally have a high standard deviation as the stock will move rapidly up and down throughout the year. Both investments may conceivably produce the same return in a given year, but one may have higher highs and lower lows, while the other may be slow and steady. This is an important concept for you to understand as you are considering various investment options. Too much volatility can lead to emotional decisions regarding your investment holdings.

The following chart shows two investments, both of which start with $1,000 and end with $1,066. While the annual return on the investments is the same, the standard deviations are radically different. One is not inherently better than the other, but the investor should understand the likely volatility of an investment prior to purchasing it.

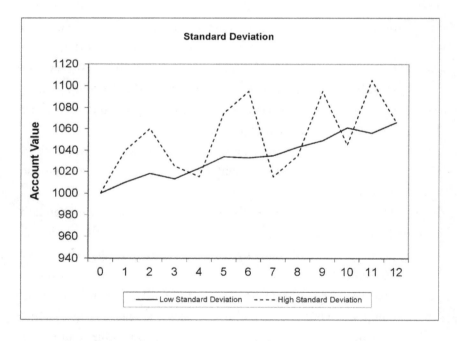

Investments with high standard deviations will result in more of a roller-coaster ride for your portfolio. If this ride would cause you to jump off instead, consider investments with a lower standard deviation.

- Next, let's define "dollar cost averaging" or DCA (McWhinney 2019), a term you'll often see used in the personal financial community. Quite simply, DCA is the investment of a fixed amount on a regular schedule. Whether the market is up or down, you continue to invest the same amount. When prices are up, the amount invested buys fewer shares. However, when the stock market drops, the fixed monthly contribution you are making buys more shares. This has the effect of reducing your average share cost and will cushion the blow of a large market drop by buying shares "on sale." DCA is also helpful for reducing the temptation to try and time the market, or sell in fear when the next market correction occurs. The most common form of DCA is the typical 401k or 403b plan. Fixed amounts are withheld from your paycheck and invested routinely, whether the market is up or down. Dollar cost averaging is an excellent tool to build long-term wealth!

- A final concept to understand is average returns vs. the more accurate compound annual growth rate, otherwise known as *CAGR*. Often, mutual funds will advertise an impressive annual growth rate, and mathematically, they would be correct. However, this statistic can be misleading if you don't understand how it's calculated. CAGR tries to present the investment return more accurately.

  This is best illustrated by an example. Suppose a mutual fund's price goes from $10.00 to $20.00 during year one. You'd be accurate to say the fund had a 100% return for that year. Suppose, in year two, the fund goes from $20.00 per share back to $10.00 per share. It would be accurate to say the fund suffered a 50% loss for the year. Averaging the 100% positive return from year one with the 50% negative return from year two would show an *average* return of 25%. However, you are left with the same $10.00 you had at the beginning of year one, so your total return is actually zero. In this example, the CAGR for this investment would be zero, accurately reflecting the investments actual two-year return. CAGR is not the actual return for each year, of course, but the "imaginary number that describes the rate at which an investment would have grown if it grew at a steady rate" (Murphy 2019). Keep this in mind as you review the various investment options you're considering.

Investing Principles

With this background in mind, let's consider several principles for solid investing that can be easily adopted and implemented in your investment plans. These principles should form the backbone of your investment strategy.

1. Diversification

As we've already seen earlier, no one can accurately predict the success of one segment of the market over any other segment. Therefore, diversification across the entire market is the solution to this problem. Ecclesiastes 11:2 (NKJV) reminds us to "Give a serving to seven, and also to eight, for you do not know what evil will be on the earth."

History has shown, and it was documented earlier, that the "hot" market segment changes practically every year. The strategy of selecting only certain market segments in which to invest requires constant review of your investment portfolio. Realistically, most investors will not perform these reviews. Even if an investor does watch the markets closely, they will be wrong more than they are right. If investing professionals constantly underperform the overall market, it's unrealistic to believe the average investor will do better. Remember the advice found in Ecclesiastes 11:6 (NKJV): "In the morning sow your seed, and in the evening do not withhold your hand; *for you do not know which will prosper, either this or that, or whether both alike will be good.*" A well-diversified portfolio allows investors to pursue other interests in life while still being able to participate in the better performing sectors.

Principle: Diversify your investments to cover a wide range of market sectors.

Examples of well-diversified mutual funds include: Vanguard Total Stock Market Index Fund (Fund Symbol VTSAX); Vanguard Total International Stock Index Fund (Fund Symbol VTIAX); and Vanguard Total Bond Market Index Fund (Fund Symbol VBTLX).

2. Control costs and taxes

As we all know, no one can control the performance of the marketplace. However, we're not totally powerless to have some positive influence on our investment results. There are two primary factors over which we do have some measure of control: costs and taxes.

The costs of investments that we choose can vary significantly. A well-diversified index fund may have costs as low as 0.04%.[11] Some fund families are now offering index funds with no management fee. As explained earlier, actively managed mutual funds typically have management expenses significantly higher. In 2012, the average actively managed US equity fund had an expense ratio of 1.232% (Lipper Alpha Insight 2013). Over time, this seemingly small expense difference will have a significant impact on the value of your portfolio. For example, a report published by Vanguard showed that over a thirty-year investment period, a single $100,000 investment which returned 6% annually would have a value of $532,889 if the expense ratio was 0.25%. This same investment would be worth only $438,976 if the expense ratio was 0.90%, a difference of $93,913 (Vanguard n.d.).

I developed a spreadsheet for use with my counseling clients which showed the compound impact of costs over a longer period of time. My assumptions were: $100,000 beginning balance, an 8% annual return and $12,000 in annual additions for thirty years. This would very much mirror a married couple's contributions to a Roth IRA over their working career.

If the fund had an expense ratio of 0.10% (which is higher than many

---

[11] Expense ratio for Vanguard Total Stock Market Index Fund Admiral Shares (VTSAX). The ETF version of the same fund has an expense ratio of only 0.03%.

index funds), the investment would grow to $2,313,399 at the end of thirty years. If the fund had an expense ratio of 1.10% (which is lower than many actively managed funds), the investment would have grown to only $1,853,508, a reduction of nearly $460,000! Expenses matter a great deal over time—keep your costs low.

Additionally, some funds charge a load (or fee) to purchase or to sell them. For example, a 5% sales load would mean the mutual fund managers would keep 5% of what you invest for themselves, and invest only the remaining 95% in the fund you select. Some funds charge a load on the "back end," or when you sell the fund. These loads (or fees) are *in addition to* ongoing annual management fees. With so many excellent "no-load" funds available today, there is no reason to pay a load!

An additional cost that you can strongly influence is taxes. As mentioned earlier, your choice of account type will determine whether you'll have to claim income from an investment when it's earned. Many investors will incorrectly place bond funds in taxable accounts while leaving funds that may be more tax efficient in tax-preferred accounts such as an IRA or 401k.

While these costs may be small, the compound effect over time is significant. As shown above in regards to the fund expenses, even a small tax cost can have a significant long-term impact on your portfolio. Taxes are a part of life, but should be minimized whenever legally possible.

Principle: Keep your investing costs and tax costs as low as possible.

3. Use no-load index funds vs. actively managed funds or individual stocks

To achieve the diversification and the low cost we've already set as our priorities above, the most efficient way to do that is through no-load index funds. To review the earlier explanation, these funds simply strive to match the performance of whatever they are indexed to. For example, an S&P 500 index fund merely tries to mimic the results of the S&P 500. Since the fund managers are only mirroring an index, it's much less costly for them to manage the fund. They don't need to spend resources investigating investment options trying to outperform the market, as actively managed funds attempt to achieve. They are striving to outperform the market by selecting securities that they believe will beat the market return in the next period. But as we've already seen, it's unrealistic to expect any manager to *consistently* outperform the market when the top performing asset classes are constantly changing in unpredictable ways.

While low-cost index funds have some small management fees associated with them, to avoid these fees, some investors consider purchasing individual stocks on their own. This, too, is a bad idea for most investors. The Vanguard Total Stock Index Fund holds over 3,600 different securities.[12] That level of diversification minimizes the significance of a loss should any individual security become worthless. Should you decide to purchase individual stocks, simply holding twenty, thirty, or forty individual securities is not proper diversification. The loss of even a single stock in a portfolio of that size would have a material effect. Further, the research needed to profitably invest in individual stocks is not just prior to purchase. You'll need to constantly research each of the companies in which you're invested to make sure that nothing negative has happened. There's a reason mutual funds charge a management fee to watch over the stocks that they hold. It's because it takes time and expertise to manage—time you'll have to invest if you're purchasing individual stocks.

The positive consequences of using low-cost index funds can be seen in the indisputable results. For the fifteen-year period ending June 30, 2018, large cap index funds outperformed 92.43% of their actively managed counterparts (Perry 2018). Mid-cap index funds outperformed 95.13% and small cap index funds outperformed 97.70% of their respective actively managed competitors (Perry 2018). A few lucky active managers may outperform the index in any particular year, but the

---

[12] Per Vanguard.com, for the Vanguard Total Stock Index Fund (VTSAX) as of April 30, 2019.

probability of successfully picking which active manager will do so for upcoming years is near zero. Better to consistently be in the 92-to-94 percentile than to try and predict tomorrow's successful fund managers.

Low-cost index funds offer diversification at a much lower cost than actively managed funds and are the best investment vehicle for the vast majority of investors.

Principle: Low-cost index mutual funds are the most efficient means to investing in the market.

4. Stay the course

There are no *legitimate* get-rich-quick schemes when it comes to investing. Sometimes people seem to act like there's some magic that they are unaware of...some secret to successful investing. Truthfully, there isn't. Successful investing comes from starting as early as possible, saving as much as possible, keeping costs and taxes low, and diversifying holdings across as many companies and sectors as possible.

Don't fall for schemes that promise outsized returns with minimal risk. It simply doesn't exist. If it did, those hawking such plans would spend their time investing in them, not trying to sell them to you. Remember (as mentioned earlier), risk and return are always linked. *High* return equals *high* risk. *Low* risk equals *low* return.

The most successful long-term investors are those that stay the course. One of the critical mistakes uncommitted investors make is to sell when the market drops (thus locking in your losses), and then only reentering the market when they feel comfortable. Such a feeling usually comes after the market has stabilized and shown significant increases. Buying then will mean you've missed all of those gains.

A classic, albeit extreme, example of moving in and out of the market revolved around the CGM Focus mutual fund. This extremely risky large cap value fund had a total annual return of 17.84% over the ten years ending July 31, 2009. $10,000 invested at the beginning of this period would have been worth $51,633 as of July 31, 2009. However, the actual investors of the fund suffered a loss of (16.82%) per year during the same ten-year period! So, $10,000 first invested on August 1, 1999 would have been worth $1,585 on July 31, 2009. What caused this dramatic difference? Actual investors continually moved into and out of the mutual fund as its price moved up and down. They bought when its price spiked, then sold when it sunk again. "The difference—all $50,048 worth—is attributable to investors repeatedly mistiming their purchases and sales in *chasing performance*" (Haig 2009).

A more typical experience is found in a study that showed for the twenty-year period ending December 31, 2015, the S&P 500 Index (large US companies) averaged returns of 9.85% per year. Average returns for equity investors during the same period was only 5.19% per year (Anspach 2019). More evidence that constant trading leads to under-performance. An axiom I like to remember is, "Your investments are like a bar of soap. The more you touch it, the smaller it gets!"

Staying the course doesn't mean that you *never* make changes to your portfolio, such as lowering your equity allocation as you age. It means that you set a course and make changes based on logical reasons (like changes in your circumstances), not due to an emotional reaction to the market.

Principle: Investing is for the long-term, so stay the course.

5. *Invest for the "total return"—don't choose investments based on their dividends*

In the low-interest rate environment of the last several years, the popularity of owning dividend paying stocks or mutual funds has grown significantly. The justifications for choosing dividend paying investments include claims like these:

- "Interest bearing investments, like savings accounts, money market funds, and bond holdings pay rates below what many "high-yielding" stocks, mutual funds, or ETFs do, so invest in dividend paying stocks instead of the low-yielding accounts."

- "Dividends are like 'free money.' You still own just as many shares as you did before."
- "You're not spending your capital when you limit your withdrawals to the dividends collected."
- "The dividends paid per share has grown annually for many 'dividend aristocrat'[13] stocks. This is an increase in your income every year!"

Upon closer examination, however, these statements are inaccurate. To see why, let's consider what happens when a company declares a dividend by looking at an extremely simple example. Publicly traded companies are, of course, far more complex, but this example will show the error in the "dividend investing" scheme.

Suppose Company ABC has only ten shares of stock and you own them all. They have $100 in the bank and no other assets or debts. Therefore, each share is worth $10 ($100 in the bank divided by ten shares) and your investment is worth $100. Company ABC then declares a dividend of $1.00 per share. When the company distributes the dividend, you will receive $10 ($1.00 per share for each of the ten shares that you own). The company now has only $90 in the bank. Remember: the "free money" had to come from somewhere, and in this case, it was from the bank account of Company ABC. As stated earlier, before the dividend, your investment was worth $100. After the dividend, your investment is worth $90, plus you have $10 in cash for a total asset value of…$100. There is no change in the value of what you own! You simply move from $100 in stock to $90 in stock and $10 in cash.

Suppose instead that Company ABC doesn't declare a dividend, but you need $10 to pay some personal bills. Since there is no dividend

---

[13] Dividend aristocrat companies are those that have increased the annual dividend distribution per share for at least twenty-five consecutive years. A few examples (as of the date of publishing) include McDonalds and Chevron.

income to receive, you decide to sell one share to someone else for the per share value of $10. After the sale, you now own nine shares at $10 apiece, plus the $10 you received from selling the one share. Remember: the company didn't spend any of its money. It still has $100 in the bank, but you only own 90% of the company.

Under both scenarios (a dividend payout and a sale of one share), you end up with $90 in stock and $10 in cash. There is no free money! Neither scenario puts you ahead of the other.

Some may argue that you get better tax treatment with a dividend if the investments are held in a taxable brokerage account[14]. In truth, the tax liability is exactly the same if a couple of very common conditions are met. They are:

- The dividends received must be "qualified dividends," and
- The share sold must have been owned for over one year (considered "long-term capital gains" ("LTCG")).

"Qualified dividends" are those paid by a US or a qualified foreign company that are not from specifically excluded classifications,[15] and that you've owned for the required holding period[16]. This covers the vast majority of dividends paid annually. Qualified dividends and LTCGs are, under current law, taxed at the same rates!

Limiting your investments to securities that pay a dividend restricts the number of companies in which you'd invest which, in turn, limits the amount of diversification. As previously discussed, a wide diversification is required to lessen the severity of having too much invested

---

[14] Investments held in a traditional retirement account (such as an IRA or a 401k plan at work) are not taxed until the funds are withdrawn from the account. Transactions occurring within the retirement account typically have no impact on your taxes when they are made (as long as the funds stay within the account).

[15] Such as Real Estate Investment Trusts (REIT) or Business Development Companies (BDC), for example. Tax law requires special treatment of certain types of dividends.

[16] The 121-day period starting sixty days before the dividend is declared and ending sixty days after the dividend is declared. The date of the dividend is the 121st day.

in one company or sector. Instead, always invest for "total return." The formula for "total return" is simple: ***Total return = Dividends + Stock Price Growth***. So, for example, if a company paid 1% in dividends this year and the stock price grew by 7% in the same year, your ***total*** return is 8%. You may reinvest the dividend if you don't need the cash, or you can sell some of your shares (which are worth 7% more than last year in this example) to raise additional cash.

A tax advantage of using a total return approach is additional tax flexibility. You will ***not*** control when a company declares a dividend or how much will be distributed. However, you will have to declare the dividend as income and pay the appropriate taxes due. You ***can*** control when you sell an investment. If you don't sell any shares, there is nothing to report and no taxes to pay.

There is no reason to chase dividends and limit the companies in which you can invest. Instead, think "total return" and open up the full range of diversification.

6. *Avoid the temptation to "get rich quick"*

If you're trying to make a killing in the market, you're speculating, or what I call gambling. It's a surefire way to lose money. Proverbs 13:11 (NLT) reminds us that "Wealth from get-rich-quick schemes quickly disappears; wealth from hard work grows over time."

Investing is a "win-win" proposition. The company you invest in wins by using your money to build the company, increase sales, and employ workers. You win by reaping a share of their growing profits. Gambling is "get rich quick" by means of a "hot stock pick," supposed "insider information" (which is typically illegal to profit from), or new type of investment (for example, Bitcoin). Avoid the temptation to invest this way.

I'm always amused as the end of a year approaches and I start to see the various predictions about which investment is poised for a breakout performance the next year. It seems everyone has an opinion. Rarely do

I see, however, an analysis of the previous year's predictions. Probably because so few of the predictions come true.

Remember the earlier chart showing the returns of various types of investments over time. History clearly shows us that there is no way to accurately—and consistently—predict which type of investment will top the others, and trying to do so is speculation.

Think of it this way: with nine investment types shown in the earlier chart, there is an 11.1% chance of guessing the top performer in Year 1. There is a 1.23% chance of picking the top performers for both Year 1 and Year 2. After just five years (not the twenty years shown in the table), someone would have only a 0.001% chance of accurately predicting all five years. To put those odds in perspective, a gambler has around a 1% chance of winning six hands of blackjack in a row. If your odds in Las Vegas are 1,000% better than your investment plan, you may need to rethink your strategy.

God expects us to work, not try to get rich quick. In Luke 12:15, Jesus said, "Watch out! Be on your guard against all kinds of greed." I think attempts to "get rich quick" would fall under this warning.

7. *Periodically rebalance your portfolio*

Over time, your original asset allocation will become unbalanced because the returns of the individual investments vary. For example, an investor may begin the year with 60% allocated to the Vanguard Total Stock Market Index Fund and 40% allocated to the Vanguard Short Term Corporate Bond Fund. As the year unfolds, the stock fund may perform better than the bond fund. By December of that year, the stock fund may have increased to 65% of the total portfolio value, while the bond fund has been reduced to 35% of the total value. Adopting the policy of annual rebalancing would require the investor to sell a portion of the stock fund and purchase the bond fund with the proceeds in an amount sufficient to bring the total portfolio back to the 60% – 40% allocation originally desired.

What are the benefits of doing this? First, bringing the portfolio allocation back to an acceptable level of risk prevents it from taking on too much risk for your comfort. Recall the chart earlier that shows increasing volatility in a portfolio as the equity investment increases. Over time, history has shown that stock funds outperform bond funds. If there was no rebalancing taking place, years later, the investor may have a significantly higher percentage of stock funds than desired. As discussed earlier, this portfolio now has more risk than the investors are willing to incur. Rebalancing helps prevent this from happening.

Secondly, rebalancing forces the investor to buy low and sell high. By selling the sector that has done well (and is thus overweighted) the investor is locking in some of these gains. By taking the proceeds from that sale and buying the sector that has underperformed, the investor is buying when prices are lower. Both of these are positive long-term steps.

Studies have shown that regular rebalancing offers a higher return and lower risk than leaving the portfolio unbalanced.

One word of caution: If you rebalance within a taxable account, the sale of securities will be a taxable event. For this reason, rebalancing should generally be performed inside of a tax preferred account (such as an IRA or 401k). Be sure to understand the tax implications if you sell a security in a taxable account. If it's being sold at a loss, it may be fine to sell and realize a tax savings. However, if it's being sold at a gain, you will have to recognize the income. Consult a tax advisor if you're unsure of the tax cost or implications.

While there is some debate within the investing community as to how to deal with rebalancing, I believe periodic rebalancing is an important step for every investor. Assets should be rebalanced at least once per year and no more than quarterly.

Principle: Rebalance to keep your asset allocation correct.

8. Include foreign holdings in your portfolio

In 1975, the United States stock market represented 52% of the global stock market. By 2013, the US stock market represented just 36%

of the worldwide investment opportunities, and by 2030, it is projected to be only 30%. As such, it makes sense to include these investment opportunities in your portfolio. By adding investments in foreign companies, your portfolio will have additional diversification.

Fortunately, there are low-cost index mutual funds available for this type of investment. An excellent example is the Vanguard Total International Stock Index Fund (Fund Symbol VGTSX).

I would recommend against the inclusion of foreign bonds in your portfolio for several reasons. First, some foreign bond funds are not hedged for currency fluctuations, which makes them riskier. Second, they are more expensive to invest in than domestic bonds. And finally, recall that bonds are for security, not for a great return. Domestic bonds provide this stability.

9. *Ignore the so-called "experts" predictions about the future*

I place little weight on so-called "experts" predictions for the future and I certainly would not change my investments based on them. Too many unpredictable events in the economic and political environment may occur that would radically change the investing world. Further, they are often wrong, sometimes spectacularly so.

For example, Barron's reported in December 2007 that *all of the analysts* they surveyed predicted "higher stock prices in 2008, although their estimated gains vary widely, from 3% to 18%. On average, the group sees the Standard & Poor's 500 at 1,640 by the end of next year, or about 10% higher than the recent 1,486 with global growth and a benevolent Federal Reserve serving as twin crutches for the aging bull" (Tan 2007). Of course, hindsight tells us that *all of them were wrong* as the S&P 500 lost 37% in 2008. Case closed.

Create a well-thought-out plan based on your individual situation and ignore the noise from Wall Street, television, and the Internet. They are there to sell products or advertising, not grow your wealth.

Action Plan for Successful Investing

Having discussed the principles of investing, what should the new investor do next? Here are your action steps to take:

- Determine the risk profile that offers the best historical return *for which you'd be willing to suffer the "worst" historical losses* (refer to the allocation chart provided earlier). ***Be realistic!*** Don't assume you can take a high level of risk simply to secure a higher expected return. If you invest in too risky a portfolio, you'll sell your investments during a market correction, locking in your losses. It's better to earn a lower expected return and stay invested even during the down times than it is to reach beyond your risk tolerance and sell when the market drops.

- Determine the asset allocation that most closely matches the risk profile you've determined is acceptable. Keep costs in mind. First, decide on the allocation for the portfolio as a whole (for all of your investment accounts—IRAs, 401ks, and taxable accounts). Then allocate the investments to the various account types (taxable, IRA, 401k, and Roth IRA) you may have available based on the best tax treatment. Each individual account doesn't have to have the same percentage of each mutual fund. For example, all of the bond mutual funds should be in tax-preferred accounts (IRA/401k) if possible. Low dividend investments, like the Vanguard Total Stock Market Index Fund, would be a great option if you have a taxable account.

- Determine your rebalancing timetable. Most investors schedule their rebalancing once per year. This is probably sufficient for virtually all investors. Some only rebalance every two or three years, while others may do so twice a year. Pick a timeframe that works for you, but make sure the step is taken regularly.

- Develop an Investment Policy Statement (IPS). This is simply a written plan that specifies your investment strategy. The benefit of having such a written plan is that it reduces the emotional reaction most investors, including myself, have when the market may go through a period of increased volatility. Human nature calls for most of us to "do something" in the face of a rapid market fall, but history has shown this is almost always the wrong thing to do. Having a *written plan* will encourage you to stay the course. Included in Appendix A is an example of such an IPS. Don't copy it for your own use. You must make your IPS personally for you!

Investing Frequently Asked Questions (FAQs)

Listed below are investing related Frequently Asked Questions (FAQs) that I routinely receive.

- *How do I choose an advisor if I'm not comfortable managing my own investments?*

In most cases, adopting an investing strategy as described in this chapter allows an investor to manage their own portfolio. By limiting the chosen investments to low-cost index funds, the only ongoing management is to periodically review your comfort with risk, and then rebalance accordingly.

Some investors, though, would feel better including the services of an investment professional. The Scripture does encourage us to seek wise advice when needed. Proverbs 15:22 states, "Plans fail for lack of counsel, but with many advisers they succeed." The problem is determining who you can trust, which type of services is right for you, and how much you should pay for those services.

Fortunately, today's investing environment offers us more affordable options than ever before. Should you decide to seek help from an advisor, here are a few suggestions to consider:

a) **Only work with a fiduciary.** These individuals must put your interest above their own as they make recommendations. Ask them to confirm that they are a fiduciary **100% of the time**[17] (some act as a fiduciary only in certain areas). Ask for a copy of their Form ADV, which is required for professional investment advisors to file annually with the Securities and Exchange Commission (SEC). This form will list any disciplinary action against the advisor (Part 1), as well as disclose how they are paid (Part 2).

b) **Use an advisor that charges by the hour.** Do not use an advisor that is paid by commission as that model may sway their advice and is expensive. Do not use an advisor that charges a percentage of your account balance every year (called an "asset under management" [AUM] fee). You pay your doctor, lawyer, and accountant, among others, by an hourly rate. Your investment professional should be the same.

c) **Interview at least three fiduciary, fee-only advisors.** It's important to find an advisor with whom you are comfortable working. If you're married, both spouses should participate in this process. When one of you passes away, the surviving spouse should be comfortable working with the advisor.

• *Is my risk tolerance the only view of risk that I need to consider?*

Earlier, the subject of risk tolerance was briefly discussed. Risk, however, encompasses more than just your tolerance. It also involves your risk capacity and risk need. Let's look at all three types of risk to understand how they fit into the creation of a proper investment portfolio.

Investing Risk #1: Tolerance – **Underlying question:** *How should I allocate my portfolio into stocks versus bonds?*

This is, of course, a logical question to ask before one begins to invest. Most investors understand that risk plays a role in the development of their investment strategy. As mentioned previously, there are many free risk tolerance assessment tools available. A quick Google search on the term

---

[17] As a licensed Certified Public Accountant (CPA), I am required to act as a fiduciary at all times.

"risk questionnaire" returned over 67,000,000 results, although I doubt all of them are helpful. Stick with well-known investment companies, like Vanguard for example, when taking risk tolerance questionnaires.

Typically, you will be asked about your investing time frame, your comfort with falling markets, and your experience as an investor. Further, you're asked how you may react (or did react) if the market suffered a significant downward correction like we experienced in 2001 and 2008. Based on your answers, you'll be provided with an estimate of how you should break down your investment portfolio between stocks and bonds. The more risk you can handle, the higher the allocation to stocks. Likewise, if you're susceptible to panic selling in a crisis, the calculator should recommend a larger allocation to bonds.

They can help give you an idea of where to start when deciding how much to put into stocks versus bonds, but offer an incomplete view of risk.

Investing Risk #2: Capacity – **Underlying question:** *Can I afford to take investment risk?*

Risk considerations go beyond a simple stock/bond breakdown. Can you **afford** to take the risk that a tolerance questionnaire recommends? How do you know?

Risk capacity analysis centers on our ability to lose a portion of the funds we already have and not suffer an immediate financial crisis. For example, suppose you have a total of $10,000 saved. You can't afford to lose half of the amount in a market meltdown. Your margin for loss is too small.

The measuring tool I recommend for assessing your risk capacity is to consider whether you have a sufficient emergency fund for your financial situation (discussed in Chapter 7). Having the appropriate amount of contingency money in a money market or savings account creates the capacity to take on risk with your pot of investing money!

Imagine a 2001 or 2008 meltdown happening just as your roof springs a leak or your car needs a major repair. Instead of being able to leave your investments alone, you would be forced to sell your holdings to raise the needed funds. Since the share price would be much lower, you would need to sell even more of the shares to raise the same amount of money. Each share sold is one less share to earn back some of your losses when the market inevitably recovers. You've locked in the losses!

***Investing Risk #3: Need* – Underlying question:** *How much investing risk do I need to take on to meet my financial goals?*

Will you always need to subject your investments to the same amount of risk? In my opinion, the answer is no. Assume, for example, that your risk tolerance questionnaire indicated that your allocation should be 70% stocks and 30% bonds. Further, assume that you have accumulated a large nest egg relative to your spending needs in retirement. Should your allocation stay at 70%/30%?

Here again is the chart provided earlier that shows the average returns for various stock/bond allocations:

Allocation		Average	Best	Worst
Stocks	**Bonds**	**Return**	**Return**	**Return**
100%	0%	10.00%	54.20%	-43.10%
90%	10%	9.70%	49.80%	-39.00%
80%	20%	9.40%	45.40%	-34.90%
70%	30%	9.10%	41.10%	-30.70%
60%	40%	8.70%	36.70%	-26.60%
50%	*50%*	*8.30%*	*32.30%*	*-22.50%*
40%	60%	7.80%	27.90%	-18.40%
30%	70%	7.30%	28.40%	-14.20%
20%	80%	6.70%	29.80%	-10.10%
10%	90%	6.20%	31.20%	-8.20%
0%	100%	5.50%	32.60%	-8.10%

Note that the average annual return is 5.5% for a 100% bond portfolio, while the 100% stock allocation grew at 10.0% annually. Let's go back to our example above. Suppose you find that your portfolio only needs 8.25% growth in order to meet your spending needs in retirement. You could then move to a 50%/50% allocation (bold line in the chart) instead of your natural 70%/30% split and still meet your growth needs. Doing so will lessen the damage done to your nest egg when (not if) the next market correction occurs.

Consider this investing truth: When you've won the game, stop playing! Translated for our example above: Why take on risk that you don't need to face? For this very reason, my personal retirement portfolio is at a more conservative allocation than my risk tolerance would deem appropriate. If we did not consider our need for risk, we would be exposing our portfolio to larger potential losses than necessary to meet our long-term financial goals.

As you consider your risk profile, don't limit your analysis to simply completing a few risk tolerance questionnaires. That is a great place to start! You'd be wise to also consider your risk capacity and your risk need. Take the time to make sure your portfolio matches not just your risk personality, but also your financial condition.

- *If one of my investments is down, should I keep it until it breaks even, or should I sell it and move on?*

If you're following the investment advice in this chapter, you can avoid this question all together. Your portfolio should only consist of a few low-cost index funds and the only buy/sell decision that needs to be made is when it's time to rebalance the portfolio or you've had a significant life change that requires an adjustment to your portfolio.

However, if you own various funds and/or individual stocks, this question becomes relevant. While I don't endorse the idea of owning such funds or stocks, if you've decided to include them in your portfolio, then my recommendation is to ignore what you paid for the holding. It's irrelevant. What matters is where is the best place to invest for the future. Ask yourself if you would repurchase the same security today at its current price. If you would, hold on to it. If you would not, then sell it and buy what you prefer. Many investors hold on to poorly performing securities waiting to recover their original investment. Meanwhile, they've missed out on better performing sectors.

To be clear again, I do not recommend investing (or gambling) in this manner, but if you do so, always evaluate your portfolio by asking if you'd repurchase the same shares. Of course, be sure to take taxes into consideration if you own the security in a taxable brokerage account. Even better, skip this strategy and buy index funds instead!

- *Are index funds considered "Biblically Responsible Investing" (BRI)?*

One of the difficulties of BRI is the lack of a uniform definition and application. There is no one standard for what qualifies as BRI. For example, most would clearly agree that purchasing the stock of companies in the casino, alcohol, or pornography industry would not qualify as BRI. How about government bonds? Do they qualify as BRI? Some would say they do, but why, for example, does the federal government issue bonds? They issue bonds to finance their expenditures through debt. The Heritage Foundation reported that Planned Parenthood received over $1.5 billion in taxpayer funds from 2013 to 2015 (Burke 2018). Obviously, a portion of this amount was financed with government debt, as was a portion of all government spending. Therefore, some government debt provided financing for the largest abortion provider of the world. Does that sound like BRI to you?

There is a strong argument to be made that Christians *shouldn't* automatically divest their holdings of companies adopting policies that run counter to Scripture. Matthew 5:13-16 challenges believers to be salt and light in our world. Our light is to shine before others, bringing attention and glory to God. If Christians disengage from certain companies due to their management decisions, how can believers influence them to reconsider their positions?

Ownership of a public company, even a small percentage, provides opportunities for addressing issues important to Christians. Stock ownership brings with it the right to attend annual meetings, as well as to vote on many issues and the Board of Directors. A relatively small but vocal percentage of shareholders have coaxed Boards toward a "progressive" stand on many issues. A small but vocal percentage of Christian share-holders may be able to coax a move in a Biblical direction, too. The odds may be small, but they are even smaller if we (as Christians) abandon any association with progressive publicly traded companies.

I've prayerfully considered this issue and am at peace with using index funds. I understand that some of the companies in the index are ones that I would not purchase if I was selecting individual stocks. Unfortunately, today's economy is so complex and intertwined that it's difficult if not impossible to select investments that are 100% BRI, especially with so many definitions of "BRI" that exist.

Personally, I like using some of my investment gains to support ministries that strive to counter the actions of non-BRI companies. For my personal spending, I may refuse to patronize a company that openly adopts policies that clearly counter Christian teaching. I'm of the opinion that Christians joining together to boycott company's hostile to our faith will get the attention of their management faster than if I refused to buy a few of their publicly traded shares. I consider it a decision to be "Biblically Responsible Spending" (BRS) instead of BRI.

I would encourage every Christian to prayerfully consider how they handle every aspect of their stewardship responsibilities, including how to invest (BRI) and spend (BRS).

Closing Thoughts

My goal with this chapter is to educate you to make well-thought decisions regarding how to invest. Obviously, we don't cover every subject possible, but for a majority of investors, following the guidelines and steps described here will set you well on your way to a successful investing experience.

No one can guarantee an investor a great return, and we all take some amount of risk when we invest. The point is not to avoid all risk, but to take measured risks that are appropriate for us individually. If we all had the same risk tolerance, one model portfolio could be developed for us all to use. But this is simply not the case. So, empower yourself with the knowledge used by successful investors everywhere, and begin your journey to investing success today.

One final piece of biblical advice when it comes to investing. Proverbs 23:4 counsels us to "not wear yourself out to get rich; do not trust your own cleverness." Don't try to figure out some "secret" to getting rich! Instead, simply be the best steward that you can and keep your eyes on Christ, not your investment portfolio.

Commit to growing God's wealth in God's ways. It's never too late to begin making wise decisions about your investments. Are you ready to do so?

CHAPTER 7
_____

REMOVE UNNECESSARY RISK

The prudent see danger and take refuge, but the
simple keep going and pay the penalty.

PROVERBS 27:12

There are surely many things in life that we can't avoid. An unexpected illness or job loss. A serious accident at work or while traveling. As we saw in 2008, even a worldwide economic downturn can happen at any time and impact your financial life. Fortunately for Christians, our trust is placed in an eternal, all-knowing God, not a fragile financial system.

The good news is there are many risks that we can manage or eliminate. Doing so is not only wise, but scriptural. Failing to take reasonable steps to manage risk and prepare yourself for eventual challenges can leave you and your family unprotected when a challenge comes your way. First Timothy 5:8 (NKJV) says, "But if anyone does not provide for his own, and especially for those of his household, he has denied the faith and is worse than an unbeliever." Part of that provision includes preparation for the eventual risks that will enter our lives from time to time. Again, every risk cannot be foreseen and prepared for. However, many can and should be.

Let's examine these areas where prudent planning can help us reduce or eliminate risk:

    A. Establish and maintain an adequate emergency fund

    B. Keeping your housing costs within your budget

    C. Maintain adequate insurance coverage

    D. Protect your credit profile from identity theft

    E. Reduce unnecessarily high taxes in retirement

A. *Fund and maintain an adequate emergency fund*

A fully funded emergency fund turns many financial emergencies into inconveniences. I'd still rather avoid them, of course, but an inconvenience is much different emotionally and spiritually than an emergency. The emergency fund is the single most significant way to reduce risk as it can be applied to any number of sudden needs that may arise. Let's review some basic questions to understand this vital step.

Q. What is an emergency fund and why do I need one?

An emergency fund is simply an amount of money set aside for financial difficulties that may arise. While the exact nature and timing of an emergency is unknown, we can be certain that **one will eventually arise**. It would be wise to have funds set aside to deal with it quickly and easily.

Q. Why are emergency funds so important?

One of the principles of financial stewardship is being as prepared as possible for the unexpected. That's what the Scripture refers to in Proverbs 27:12: "The prudent see danger and take refuge, but the simple keep going and pay the penalty."

If you don't have funds set aside when the need arises, the temptation will be to use credit to meet the need. Think about it: When an emergency hits, the last thing you need to do is go into debt. Sadly, many Americans struggle with funding an account for emergencies. It's been widely reported in many studies that only a small percentage of Americans could pay for a $1,000 emergency expense with available cash. The majority would have to borrow the money or cut their spending elsewhere!

Consider your emergency fund as a form of insurance—insurance against getting hit with a loss that disrupts the bigger goals you have set for your financial life. Yes, the earnings on this fund will be small, but it's not an investment—it's insurance.

Q. When should I fund one?

If you have consumer debt like credit cards, car loans, and the like, it's generally better to pay those off as quickly as possible. They often come with heavy interest costs and in all cases, they serve to siphon a percentage of your income away from giving and wealth building. Taking the time to first set aside a large emergency fund will probably slow that process down significantly. This, in turn, will possibly cost you significant additional interest charges and significantly push back any "debt-free" goal you may have in mind.

Even if you are in consumer debt, I like the idea of having at least some minimal amount of cash set aside, readily available, for any emergencies that come up. Remember: you don't want to add to your consumer debt at the same time you're trying to pay it off. How much is a minimal amount? Something in the neighborhood of $1,000 to $2,500 should be sufficient.

Q. Where should I keep it?

Your emergency fund should be kept separate from your regular operating funds, but still be readily available if needed. In other words, don't keep it in your checking account, but don't tie it up somewhere it can't be quickly accessed. Keeping it too handy, like in your checking account, can make it too easy to spend on a whim.

A great alternative is to use an online, FDIC-insured money market or savings account linked to your checking account. By using an online bank, depositors can usually get a higher interest rate than a "brick and mortar" bank without giving up the insurance protection. Should a need arise for some of the funds, an online transfer can be entered and the funds will appear in your checking account typically in two business days or less. That is quick enough to handle most emergencies, but slow enough to prevent spur of the moment purchases.

Others may choose to keep their emergency funds in certificates of deposit or savings accounts. This option is acceptable as long as you remember you'll probably incur an interest penalty if you need the money before it matures. Make sure you understand what, if any, penalty will apply if the CD is cashed before maturity. Also, if you use this strategy, divide the balance into multiple CDs. That will reduce the penalty incurred if you do need to break one early. Better to incur the penalty on just a portion of the emergency fund instead of the entire balance.

Do NOT invest in the stock or bond market with these funds, or in any illiquid investments that will restrict your access in times of financial need. While it's understandable to want higher returns, markets may crash just as you need the money. At the very time you need it, it may lose significant value. Remember: it is insurance, not an investment.

Q. How much should I have in my emergency fund?

Other than the question of whether to tithe on the gross or net pay,[18] this is an area of great disagreement among Christian (and non-Christian) financial pundits. It's not uncommon to find some who believe that three months of expenses is sufficient, while others recommend a year or more. But for most of us, that's a pretty big range. So, how do you know?

First, we need to define "expenses" for emergency fund purposes. Expenses in this context should be limited to the essentials and should exclude the discretionary. Essential expenses are those that must be paid on a regular basis; they are nonnegotiable, although there may be some flexibility in the amount. You must purchase food every month, but it can be hamburger instead of steak. Discretionary expenses are "wants."

---

[18]For what it's worth, I believe Christians should tithe off of their gross income. The fact that some was used to pay tax is no different than some of it being used to pay your mortgage payment or to pay for food. Your "increase" is your gross income. A tithe is 10% of your increase.

You'd like to have them but in the midst of an emergency is not the time to allocate toward them. When the emergency is over and the emergency fund is replenished, the discretionary expenditures can begin again.

Here are some examples of each:

Essential	Discretionary
Rent or house payment	Vacation
Food	Eating out
Utilities	Entertainment
Health care and insurance	Saving for retirement, college, etc.
Basic clothing	Fancy duds
Minimum payments on debt	Extra principal payments on loans

Now that we've defined the types of expenses to be included in our emergency fund calculation, let's consider how many months of these expenses we'll need. It can be tempting to simply say, "I'm conservative, so let's go with six months." Or to say, "Let's roll the dice and go for only three months." But a reasoned answer can be learned (and not simply guessed) if we examine our own personal situation.

To help you narrow that range, here are some questions to ask yourself:

Question	Three-Month Fund	Six-Month Fund
Are you a single or dual income family?	Dual	Single
Do you have kids at home?	No	Yes
Do you have multiple streams of income?[19]	Yes	No
Is your job stable?	Yes	No
Is your industry stable?	Yes	No
Is it easy to find a job in your profession?	Yes	No
Are you retired (or near retirement)?	No	Yes

---

[19] This may include, for example, a second job, a side business with multiple clients or rental property with a positive cash flow.

As you can see, there is no universal answer, and each person will respond to these questions differently. But when the answers are tallied up, you can get a feel for whether you should have three or six months, or maybe something in between.

Note: Consider the opportunity cost of over funding.

We'd all probably like the comfort of having a large amount of cash sitting available when financial trouble arrives. But make no mistake, having an emergency fund will "cost" money. Those are dollars that could be used to pay off debt, or could be invested in a product with a higher expected return. This lost income or additional interest paid on debt is called the "opportunity cost." It is an increased cost or income lost due to money being diverted to an emergency fund.

Let's see how too large of an emergency fund can slow you down in meeting your financial goals. Imagine you bring home $5,000 per month, and your monthly expenses are $4,500. First of all, congratulations, you have a positive monthly cash flow. Now imagine you are starting with zero saved and are going for an emergency fund of six months of expenses.

Here's the math: monthly expenses of $4,500 times six months equal $27,000 that is needed for your emergency fund. At $500 per month (your income of $5,000 less your monthly expenses of $4,500), it would take fifty-four months to save a fully funded emergency fund. That's four and a half years. Perhaps a smaller emergency fund is a better goal, with portions of future raises earmarked toward building the fund to a comfortable level. You will need to find the balance between the positive benefits of having "emergency" insurance and the negative opportunity cost of lost earnings on those dollars.

Closing Thoughts

I'm convinced that having an emergency fund is important for all of us. There is a peace of mind that comes from knowing that a cracked windshield, flat tire, or broken microwave won't force us to turn to debt (via a credit card) to resolve the problem. In fact, I've noticed that when you're prepared for emergencies, you tend to have less of them. Maybe it's just because they don't feel like "emergencies" anymore simply because you were prepared.

We don't need to accept some arbitrary rule about how much to save. There is no "one size fits all" emergency fund size. By going through the exercises described above, we can each calculate the size fund that's just right for us and our family.

B. *Keep your housing cost right-sized for your budget*

Home buying can be a trap. Overspending when you're purchasing a home is another risk that can, with a system in place, be eliminated. Failure to do so may result in housing costs far in excess of what our income can support, leading to financial stress and possible loss of the home in foreclosure (which we saw extensively in 2008).

Unfortunately, the best laid financial plans can self-destruct over a beautiful view from a backyard deck, a flowing open floor plan, or a luxurious master bath. We usually enter the home buying process with our budgets set and emotions in check. But as is so often the case, we spend more than intended when we started the process. So, why is the home buying process fraught with overspending?

It's Emotional

First, home buying is a very personal and emotion-filled process. Where do we want to raise our kids? Are the schools of good quality? Is the neighborhood safe? Is it convenient to work and church and other activities? These are all reasonable questions, but also very personal in nature. It's no longer just a monetary transaction. It involves your loved ones. We want the best for them. That's an admirable thought, but it can lead us to making emotional—instead of reasoned—decisions. Remember that emotions come from our heart and as Jeremiah reminds us, "The heart *is* deceitful above all *things, a*nd desperately wicked; Who can know it?" (Jeremiah 17:9 NKJV).

We Justify Our Wants

Also, we justify it with statements like:

"We'll be here a long time. We should get what we want."

Ever hear of a job change, job loss or illness changing your plans? Maybe you have another child and the house is now too small. Maybe the neighborhood changes, and not for the better.

Everyone hates moving and we vow to not do it again for a long, long time. Then suddenly, for any number of reasons, a realtor is putting a "for sale" sign on your front lawn.

"Real estate always goes up. What a great investment."

This is a common misconception. The housing crash in 2007 wiped out many homeowners and many markets have still not recovered (as of 2019) to their pre-crash "value." Real estate is like many other investments. It will typically grow in value over long periods of time, but may not do so during your period of ownership.

"They're not making any more real estate! I better buy now."

True, God's not making more real estate. But there are a lot of new houses for sale every day. In 2014, there were nearly 15,000 homes sold each day. You don't need real estate to be created. There is plenty around to be purchased and the listings are changing constantly.

"The bank said I could spend $xxx,xxx!"

Do you let the grocery store tell you how much you'll spend this week for food? Of course not. Then don't let a builder, realtor, or lender do it! It's your money and your stewardship responsibility. You prayerfully decide.

This exact situation happened to me once. I obtained a pre-approval letter from a mortgage lender prior to house shopping. When I showed it to a builder and agent (to prove I was an eligible buyer) they were both **SHOCKED** that I didn't want to spend the full amount of the pre-approval. My response was to find a different builder and agent.

In truth, we want what we want. There's nothing wrong with that until what we want isn't in God's plan for us. Trying to justify it with fancy sounding ideas and opinions doesn't change the facts.

Mortgage Math Is Not Your Friend

Finally, mortgage math often works against us. Rates are low (as this is written) and loan terms are so long that a change in price doesn't seem to have much impact in the payment. But what is the long-term impact?

Let's say you increase your loan amount by $25,000 to pay for the new sun room or upgraded kitchen. At 4% on a thirty-year loan, the monthly payment goes up "only" $119.35. That doesn't sound like too much of a financial impact. But don't stop your calculations now! Run the numbers all the way out. Thirty years of an extra $119.35 per month is a total of almost $43,000! Quite a bit more than the $25,000 you spent!

One more calculation to consider. Instead of the upgrade, suppose you invested the $119.35 per month for the same thirty years. Assuming a modest 8% long-term return, your $119.35 monthly payments would grow to nearly $178,000 over the length of the loan (thirty years).

The Cure

So, what's the cure? How do we inoculate ourselves against emotional overspending on our home?

Set your limit through a formula, not some arbitrary number

It's important to go into the buying process already certain on your budget. We know how hard it is to stick to it when you start seeing actual houses. To help us keep on budget, it's important to have a formula to define the limits. When we set a limit arbitrarily, it doesn't have the same sense of certainty that a formula provides.

Limit the monthly payment (including insurance and tax escrows) to 25% of your take home pay. Further, the loan should be a fifteen-year, fixed rate mortgage. Skip the thirty-year (and now forty-year) options. The interest rates are higher for the longer-term loans and do you really want to make 360 (or 480) payments on anything?

Skip the adjustable rate mortgages too. If rates happen to drop in the future, you can always refinance. Refinancing is much quicker and cheaper than just a few years ago. If rates rise, you'll be glad you have the fixed rate.

Set your spending limit with thought-out reasons and you're more likely to stick with it.

See your housing in the context of your life goals, not just a pretty place to live now.

As with every big financial decision, it's important to consider first how it fits into your overall life goals. For example, if your goal is early retirement in ten years, then an expensive home (with its high mortgage and maintenance costs) may prevent it from happening. Maybe God will call you to a career change, or to a dream job in another city. Does buying the house you're considering get you closer to your goal or push it farther away?

When we see things in a broader context, it helps to keep today's emotions in check. We understand that no matter how pretty the house or the view, it won't help us move closer to our bigger goals. Sometimes an emotional cold shower is just what we need to make sound financial decisions.

Consider the opportunity costs

As we saw in the earlier example, it's not just the increased interest cost and higher monthly payment you'll get with overspending. It's also what you could have done with the money instead. Don't just see the bigger house; consider the possibility of a bigger investment account balance or retiring a few years earlier too. Remember also that a larger house payment will require a larger emergency fund, meaning even more dollars will have to remain uninvested. Suddenly, you may have a change of heart about the house you're about to buy!

Start looking at property well below your budget, not at the top.

Too often, we tend to start looking at homes at the top of our budget. Then we see another option costing just a little bit more and our attention is turned to it instead. Next thing you know, the budget is blown. Instead, look first at properties 10% to 20% below your top budget amount. Then if you see some properties costing just a bit more, you can consider them without going over the amount you want to spend. You may end up with a nicer home than you originally considered, but still stay within (or under!) budget.

Closing thoughts

Buying a home doesn't have to cause a financial meltdown. Nor does it have to cost you your long-term dreams. If we enter the house buying process with a defined plan and view our wants with a long-term perspective, we can successfully purchase the right house. So, enjoy the process of looking at homes and getting excited about purchasing one. Just don't let the excitement lead you into a financial trap.

C. *Purchase and maintain adequate insurance coverage*

Health Insurance:

Of all of the various types of insurance that will be covered in this book, health insurance is the one that raises the most concern among Americans. It's understandable why. Health insurance premiums have steadily risen and are now, for many, too expensive. On top of the high premiums, deductibles and out of pocket maximums continue to rise. For many families purchasing their own coverage, between the premiums, deductible, and copayments, literally tens of thousands of dollars may be spent for health care services before the insurance company makes any substantial payments. The Affordable Care Act (ACA), informally referred to as "Obamacare," added many important features, including such features as:

- the elimination of preexisting condition limitations
- the ability for children to stay on their parent's coverage until they turn twenty-six years old
- no-cost preventative visits
- the elimination of lifetime benefit caps

Unfortunately, it has done little, if anything, to reduce the premium costs. In fact, the additional coverage requirements mandated by the ACA have contributed to the rapid growth in premium costs.

Of course, going without health insurance is a risky proposition. One unfortunate accident could wipe out any hard-earned increases in your net worth. What options do we have to help with the costs of health care?

Fortunately, the vast majority of American's receive some level of health insurance through their employer. While the coverage may not be ideal, it is normally less expensive than trying to secure coverage on your own. Additionally, seniors and low-income families are typically eligible for Medicare and Medicaid, respectively, offering affordable coverage to that segment of the population.

For others, here are some options to consider:

1. **Health Care Marketplace**[20] established by the ACA – From here, one can determine which plans are offered in their states to individuals and families seeking coverage. There are limited

---

[20] Health Care Marketplace or www.healthcare.gov for most families. Some states created their own exchange, so check with your state to determine the appropriate site to use.

times of open enrollment, so planning in advance is important so you're prepared when that period arrives. Do not wait until you need coverage to buy it. This is like trying to buy fire insurance when your house is already on fire. It's unethical to expect other insured families to subsidize your medical expenses if you haven't been paying into the same system when you were healthy.

2. **Health care sharing ministries** have also grown in popularity since the ACA was enacted. With these ministries, the members' eligible health care expenses are shared by the other ministry members. This is not considered insurance! Therefore, they are not covered by the ACA coverage mandates and will not cover the same range of services. Most of these ministries are Christian-based and therefore have lifestyle requirements (they will not, in most cases, cover claims resulting from lifestyle choices that are counter to the Scripture). My family has used one of these ministries in the past when we did not purchase traditional health insurance. Our experience was positive, but every family situation is different, especially if you have preexisting conditions. These ministries are worth considering, but please make sure you understand the rules and limitations before enrolling.

3. **Employer continuation coverage (COBRA)** may be available if you've recently left a job. Check with the human resources department of your former employer to see if it's available and if so, the monthly cost. This is often an expensive option (as the employer will typically no longer cover part of the cost), but it may be the best option if you have ongoing health needs.

4. **Trade associations** to which you may belong (or be eligible to join) may offer group health insurance plans to their members. Research whether you are eligible for any of these associations (often, they offer discounts on other types of insurance, too). Examples would be associations for small business owners, artists, writers, freelance workers, and contractors, among others.

5. **Short-term, limited coverage plans** are available in many

areas. These plans have limited benefits, but are better than going without coverage. Typically, they only offer coverage for a short period of time, but may be renewable. Check in your state to see what short-term options are available.

6. As mentioned in the opening, **Medicaid** has been expanded in most states to allow lower-income residents to participate. This, too, is provided by the states, so check with your state of residence to see if you are eligible.

Going without health insurance coverage is a dangerous proposition, and certainly not consistent with biblical instruction. Remember Proverbs 22:3: "The prudent see danger and take refuge, but the simple keep going and pay the penalty." It's naïve to believe one can go indefinitely without a way to pay for healthcare.

To help reduce the cost of health insurance, consider **increasing the deductible and/or the copayment** (the percentage of the bills you have to pay after meeting the deductible) to reduce the cost. A fully funded emergency fund (as described earlier in this chapter) can be used to cover the increased out of pocket costs if a medical emergency arises. Not ideal, certainly, but better than no coverage at all.

If you are eligible for one, consider funding a **Health Savings Account (HSA)** to allow you to pay your health care costs with pre-tax money. Contributions to an HSA are tax deductible and, if invested, they grow tax-free. When you need to reimburse yourself from the HSA for an eligible medical bill, the distribution to you is also tax-free. Unfortunately, you must be covered by an *eligible* health insurance plan in order to contribute to an HSA, so be sure to check if your plan allows contributions.

Unused HSA funds are not lost but are carried forward for use in future years. In fact, you can defer reimbursing yourself for eligible expenses and allow the account to continue to grow. Later, you can reimburse yourself—tax-free—for the old medical bills (as long as the medical service provided was after you initially opened the HSA). Each year, we collect the receipts for our out-of-pocket medical costs throughout the year, but do not get reimbursed. Instead, our HSA account is invested as discussed in Chapter 6 and continues to grow tax-free. Eventually, perhaps in retirement, we'll finally get reimbursed for those costs, which will be tax-free "income" for us at that time.

Please consider funding an HSA account if you are eligible. They are the only account that has tax deductible contributions, tax-free growth, and tax-free distributions (if the distribution is for eligible medical care expenses)!

Life Insurance:

For virtually every situation, purchasing term insurance is the appropriate way to eliminate the financial risk due to a premature death. Term insurance is inexpensive, but can provide a significant death benefit should an unfortunate event take place while the coverage is in force.

Permanent insurance (such as whole life, universal life, or variable life) are much more expensive as they need to collect extra funds to build a cash value from which to pay premiums in the future. The benefit of these policies is that they can last until death (assuming the premiums are paid in a timely manner). Most of us, though, don't need permanent coverage. We do need coverage for a period of time, during which you should be building wealth as a part of your stewardship activities. Term insurance is, by far, the least expensive option to cover the risk of death during this time of coverage need. Later, the need may be gone (ex. your children are grown, out of college, and living on their own) or the need can be funded from your personal wealth.

If you do need to replace an existing permanent insurance policy, be sure to have the new policy in place before cancelling the old policy. Failure to do so may leave you uninsured if an unknown medical issue surfaces in the underwriting process.

Purchase approximately twelve to fifteen times the amount of income you need to generate annually for a period of time (such as when the children are young). If your entire paycheck is needed, use that amount to calculate how much term insurance to purchase. Should a lesser amount be needed, base the twelve to fifteen times calculation on the lower annual need. When in doubt, round up (if you can afford it). Again, term insurance is relatively inexpensive and adding a bit more in death benefit is normally very affordable.

Regarding the length of the term for your policy, try to match the insurance policy to the amount of time your income would need to be replaced should you die prematurely. For example, if you have very young children, a policy of twenty to twenty-five years would be appropriate. After that period of time elapses, your children should be on their own and your debts should be eliminated. Your regular investing over the decades should have grown enough to provide for your spouse or heirs should you die after the policy expires. This is the strategy that I followed and my term policy has now expired and will not need to be replaced.

On the other hand, suppose your children are already grown and on their own, and you are in your mid-fifties. You plan to retire at sixty-five when your mortgage will be paid off. A term policy of only ten years may be sufficient. By then, your debts would be eliminated and you would have begun retirement (with pensions, Social Security, and investments providing the needed income).

When in doubt, go a little longer on term policy. It works great as an income replacement tool while it's needed. Hopefully you are investing regularly, as well as eliminating any outstanding debts and mortgages, so that eventually, you no longer need the policy.

Disability Insurance:

People who are younger and in the early stages of their career are often surprised to learn that they are more likely to become disabled than to die at an early age. According to the Social Security Administration, a young person is over **four times more likely to be disabled** than to die (SSA n.d.). This disability may not just eliminate their income, but may also dramatically increase their costs due to new and potentially permanent care needs.

This risk is mitigated through disability insurance. This coverage can be expensive, so look for a longer "elimination period" to reduce costs. This period is the amount of time between being declared disabled and receiving your first benefit payment. With a fully funded emergency fund, the lost income during the elimination period can be replaced. The bigger concern is being disabled for years. Therefore, cover that risk with long-term disability insurance. Often, employer plans are relatively inexpensive, but be sure to get quotes from any trade associations to which you belong, as well as your independent insurance agent (see the next section).

Do not buy short-term disability coverage as your emergency fund can be utilized to replace income for a short period of time. Some employers provide this at no cost to the employee, so, of course, enroll in that type of coverage.

Automobile, homeowners (or renters), and umbrella insurance:

For other lines of insurance, like auto and home, work with an independent agent whenever possible and review your coverages annually to make sure they fit your changing needs. An independent agent works with many different carriers and can secure several competing quotes. Some insurance companies only use "captive" agents, so you would need to work through one of them if you wanted another quote for your coverage needs. Regardless of the renewal rates, be sure to "shop" the rates at least every other year.

Liability coverage is typically relatively inexpensive. Don't simply buy the minimum required by your state. Consider raising the limits to better cover a potential loss. An umbrella policy to add to the limits of the homeowners and automobile policies are very inexpensive but offer significantly higher levels of liability coverage. As your wealth grows, so should your umbrella coverage.

Tips to consider when renewing your insurance policies

1. Use an independent agent

As discussed, some insurance companies use *"captive"* agents, meaning they can only write coverage for that one particular company. However, independent agents represent many companies simultaneously. With one call, you can request the agent to obtain quotes from many other companies. He/she will then do the work necessary to obtain the quotes. This saves the time of calling each insurance company and going over the same information time and time again.

Also, an independent agent can help when you need to file a claim. Instead of having to deal directly with the insurance companies claim adjuster, the independent agent can act as an advocate to help you with the process.

Independent agents are typically paid by the insurance company, so this service **costs you nothing, but saves you a lot of time**!

2. Start looking in a timely manner

Don't wait until your renewal date is just a few days away. Start around thirty days before your renewal date in order to have enough time to get and compare other quotes. Renewal quotes from my current carrier are typically received about this time so it's a good reminder to get the other quotes as soon as the renewal rates are received.

3. Consider higher deductibles

Another way to save on your premiums is to consider higher deductibles. Basically, this is the amount you have to pay for a covered claim before the insurance company will begin paying. Raising your deductible lessens the amount the insurance company will be obligated to pay in the event of a claim, so they reduce your premium.

Make sure you understand the premium savings associated with increasing the deductible, though. For example, raising your auto insurance deductible from $250 to $1,000 will probably save enough in premiums to make it worthwhile. Raising the deductible from $1,000 to $2,000 probably will not. Be sure the reward (in lower premiums) is worth the risk you're taking (the higher deductible).

Within a reasonable period of time you should save enough in premiums to cover the increased cost you'll incur in the event of a claim. To better explain this concept, let's consider the following example. Suppose raising your deductible from $250 to $1,000 saves you $150 in annual premium. The recovery period is then five years ($750 increase in deductible / $150/year savings = 5 years). This is a reasonable tradeoff. However, if the savings were only $50 in this example, it would take fifteen years to recover the increased deductible. This would not make sense to do as it's not worth increasing the deductible for such slim savings. The only way to know these numbers is to ask your agent to prepare the quotes with several different options.

Important point: Make sure your emergency fund is sufficient to pay the higher deductible. If you don't have adequate savings, you won't be able to pay the increased deductible without going into debt. Let this inspire you to ramp up your emergency fund as quickly as possible.

4. Consider dropping add-ons you may not need

Most insurers offer many different add-ons to their quotes—for an additional fee, of course—to cover various special and often unlikely types of claims. For example, many automobile policies offer optional coverage for things like full glass replacement, trip interruption coverage, and coverage for discs and media lost in an accident. They may be nice to have, but are they worth the extra cost? Most likely not. These "little" extras can really add up over time. Make sure you really need them. Again, having a fully funded emergency fund makes these extra coverages less necessary.

5. Review to make sure you're getting all the discounts you're entitled to

There are many discounts available. They include multipolicy, recently built home, smoke detectors, low mileage auto use, alarm systems, flood prevention devices, good student discounts, students away from home discount just to name a few. The list of discounts goes far beyond the scope of this book. Here's the point: Review your discounts with your agent. Don't be shy about asking if there are any other discounts available. It's your money! Discounts don't affect the coverage, they just affect what you pay for it!

Don't forget, too, that some groups to which you belong may offer discounts. Alumni associations, AAA, credit unions, even Costco, and some employers are excellent places to seek out additional discounts when completing your insurance renewal.

6. Check for discounts for paying a full year up front

We pay our annual premiums in full at renewal. For doing so we received an additional discount of over $200 this year. To smooth the cash flow, we use a sinking fund to set aside money throughout the year so it's ready and available at renewal. Making sure you have the funds saved in time is another big benefit of preparing a monthly budget. Both the budgeting process and sinking funds were discussed at length earlier. Go back and review those sections again, if necessary.

7. Be sure to review your homeowner's coverage limits

If you keep your homeowner's coverage in place for many years, it's easy for the value of your home to eventually exceed your coverage limit. Also, if you have made any renovations or additions to your home, the new and improved house value could easily be above your coverage limit. You don't want to find out at the time you're filing a claim that you are under-insured. "Coinsurance" (Kagan 2018) requirements found in homeowner's policies require sufficient coverage to be in place or the insurance company may reduce the amount they will pay for a covered claim.

I don't like paying premiums any more than you do, but understating the value of your property to save a few bucks is foolish. The marginal savings are incredibly slim compared to having your claim reduced due to being under-insured. Review your coverage levels with your agent to make sure you're adequately insured!

If you have any high value jewelry or collectibles, make sure you understand the coverage limits and purchase additional coverage riders if necessary. Don't assume all of your personal property is covered as there are limitations for certain property types.

8. Protect your credit score to get the best rates

Whether it's fair or not, most insurers consider your credit score when determining your premiums. They believe there is a direct relationship between how well you manage your credit and pay your bills with the likelihood of you filing an insurance claim. This relationship is so important to insurers that, as CNN reported, drivers with a poor credit history pay 91% more than those with a great credit score.

Closing thoughts

Remember, it's the job of the independent insurance broker to provide advice and expertise that we don't possess. Be open and honest in your discussions with them. Yes, they are paid by the insurance company, but they only continue to earn commissions if they take care of their clients. Insurance has, in many cases, become a commodity that can easily be obtained from any number of insurance companies and agents. Client service is important for an agent to keep his slate of business. If one is hesitant to shop your coverage among many different insurers, perhaps it's time for you to find a new agent who will.

Never just assume you're getting the best rates year after year from your current carrier. The only way to make sure you're getting the best rates is for you to take action and shop your coverage at least every other year.

D. *Guard your credit profile/prevent identity theft, including freezing your credit*

It's hard to turn on the news today and not see another story of a huge data breach. In just the last few years, there have been many huge breaches making the headlines. Here are just a few examples:

- Anthem – 2015 – 80,000,000 records
- Ebay – 2014 – 145,000,000 records
- JPMorgan Chase – 2014 – 76,000,000 records
- Home Depot – 2014 – 56,000,000 credit card records
- Target – 2013 – 40,000,000 credit card accounts and 70,000,000 customers
- Equifax – 2017 – 147,000,000 people's personal data was breached[21]
- Capital One – 2019 – 100,000,000 customer records were improperly accessed

A recent survey shows that there were 781 data breaches in the US in 2015 alone, the second highest total ever recorded. While companies housing our data try their best to protect it, data hackers present a constant threat to our information. Unfortunately, I see no reason to believe the increasing level of breaches will subside.

So, what can we do? Are we powerless to prevent our information from being stolen and misused? Actually, there are many common sense steps we can take. Of course, there are no guarantees. In today's world,

---

[21] On July 22, 2019, Equifax agreed to pay between $575 million and $700 million to settle claims related to their massive breach (per a settlement with the Federal Trade Commission, the Consumer Financial Protection Bureau (CFPB), and 50 U.S. states and territories).

it's virtually impossible to stay completely *"off the grid"*. But we can improve our odds against having our identities stolen.

Types of Identity Theft

First, let's briefly review the most common types of identity theft. I tend to first think of my credit card number or Social Security number being stolen and misused, but identity theft actually goes much deeper than just these situations.

Our federal government warns us about five primary types of identity theft:

- **Child ID theft** – Our children's IDs are especially vulnerable as the theft may easily go undetected for many years. By the time they are adults, the damage has already been done to their identities. Imagine having to go back five, ten, or more years to fix a problem.

- **Tax ID theft** – A thief uses your Social Security number to file fictitious tax returns with the Internal Revenue Service or state government. They will make up income and expense amounts in order to have a tax refund sent to them. Tax time is stressful enough without having to deal with a fraudulent return, too. Side note: This is a good reason to file your annual tax returns as soon as possible!

- **Medical ID theft** – This form of ID theft happens when your personal information, such as your Medicare ID or health insurance member number, is stolen and used to get medical services, or to issue fraudulent billing to your health insurance provider. You won't find out it happened until weeks later when your insurance company sends you an Explanation of Benefits form for services you didn't receive.

- **Senior ID theft** – Sadly, our seniors are often vulnerable to ID theft because they are in more frequent contact with medical professionals, caregivers, and staff at long-term care facilities that have access to personal information.

- **Social ID theft** – A thief uses your name, photos, and other personal information to create a phony account on a social media platform. Always be cautious about what you post on various social networking sites!

What we can do

Despite the dire statistics on the frequency of identity theft, we don't have to sit back and just wait for our turn! Here are some things we can do to stop it (or at least slow it down), and most of them are incredibly simple.

- **Keep your documents secure.** Don't carry your Social Security card in your wallet. Store your personal information in a safe and secure place at home.
- Carry only the **minimum amount of identifying information** with you and only the debit/credit cards you currently use.
- **Make copies** of the front and back of your credit cards and other items in your wallet and store them in a safe place at home. Should your wallet be stolen, this will make it much easier to quickly call the issuers and stop the damage.
- Pay attention to your **billing cycles**. If a bill doesn't arrive on time, contact the sender.
- **Review your receipts closely.** Carbon copies are rarely used, but if they are, take the carbons as well.
- **Guard your mail from theft.** Collect your mail as quickly as possible and take outgoing payments to the post office instead of using your own mail box with the flag up. This is a signal to thieves that a check may really be in the mail!
- **Shred credit card offers** received in the mail, along with old receipts, expired credit cards, account statements, and the like. "Dumpster diving" for personal information has become more prevalent.

- You can **opt out** of having pre-approved offers of credit show up in your mailbox by calling 888-5-OPT-OUT.

- Be aware of *"shoulder surfers"* when entering passwords or PIN numbers.

- **Close old credit card accounts you no longer use.** Yes, it may slightly impact your credit score. But the impact should be very small, especially when compared with the hassles that come with identity theft.

- **Keep your computer virus detection and malware software current** and scan your computer regularly. Install a firewall too.

- **Use complex passwords** online that would be hard to guess. Your mother's maiden name may not offer enough protection!

- Consider using **temporary credit card numbers** when buying online. My credit card issuer offers such a service and I take advantage of it when buying from a web site that is new to me.

- **Never respond to unsolicited emails or phone calls** requesting personal information. Fake collection calls allegedly from the IRS are very common today. Hint: The IRS will never call and demand payment. If you receive such a call, hang up immediately.

- **Order your free credit report** once a year from the three credit bureaus. You may want to stagger the reports by requesting a report from one bureau every four months.

- **Consider *"freezing"* your credit reports with the three credit bureaus.** Doing so prevents your information from going to anyone trying to open a new account. This will even preclude you from opening new accounts. If you do need to open an account, ask the potential creditor which credit bureau they use. Then "unfreeze" your account with that bureau and re-freeze it when the new account is open.

Congress passed a law—the *Economic Growth, Regulatory Relief, and Consumer Protection Act*—that requires the three credit bureaus to provide a credit freeze **at no cost to the**

consumer. The FTC posted links to those new webpages on IdentityTheft.gov. Many states already required the credit bureaus to provide free credit freezes, but it had not been a nationwide requirement, until now! This new requirement took effect September 21, 2018.

- **Consider freezing the credit profiles for your children too.** Identity theft has been reported for victims as young as one-month-old! Theft of children's identity is a growing crime and often preferred by thieves as their crimes won't be noticed until the child is an adult! These freezes are also at no cost due to the same law mentioned above.
- Finally, you may want to consider subscribing to an **identity theft protection service**. These companies will monitor your identity and assist you if you become a victim of identity theft.

What to do if you're a victim

Despite your best efforts, you may (and probably will eventually!) fall victim to identity theft.

Here's how to respond:

- **Submit a fraud alert to the three credit bureaus.** This should be free in most states as you're a victim.
- **File a complaint** with the Federal Trade Commission (FTC)
- **File a police report.** You will need this to help remove fraudulent accounts from your credit reports.
- **Contact your bank and creditors.** Using the copies of your wallet information recommended above will help with this task.
- **Create an identity theft file to contain all of the police reports, complaints, etc.** Unfortunately, you may be starting down a long and arduous road, so keeping your records complete and accessible will help.

- **Contact the Social Security Administration and the Internal Revenue Service too.** They can flag your account to be on the lookout for suspicious activity.

For more information on how to respond if you're a victim, please go to IdentityTheft.gov.

Closing Thoughts

While it can be scary to think about your identity being stolen, it isn't something we have to sit back and just wait to happen. I've been the victim of fraudulent transactions numerous times over the years despite taking steps to prevent it. While it is frustrating and time consuming to deal with, you can get through it!

Should you become a victim, **address it immediately and stay vigilant** to complete the process of reversing the damage.

E. *Reduce the risk of unnecessarily high taxes in retirement*

While it is understandable that most taxpayers focus on reducing their taxes for the current year, it's not always the best overall tax strategy. Deferring taxes indefinitely can lead to a surprising tax liability in retirement. Eventually, they will need to be paid, and it may come at a time when you're living on a lower income than you experienced in your working years.

The risk of high taxes can be reduced through prudent tax planning throughout your working career. One complicating factor is the ever-changing tax code. Congress seems to add to the complexity every year. Tax bills that become law seem to set tax rates and deductions for a period of time, but remember that a subsequent Congress can change the law at any time. Nothing is guaranteed and the same issue applies to the various state tax laws. So, while we can't know for certain what the tax laws will be when we retire, taking advantage of current tax laws, even if you're decades away from retirement, can reduce the risk of a nasty tax surprise.

Here are a few items to consider as examples. Of course, no blanket tax rules exist so your situation will certainly be different. The point of this list is to show the possibilities for tax risk reduction, at least under the current law.

- *Fully utilize the lower tax brackets* – As mentioned earlier, taxpayers understandably want to reduce their current tax liability. Why pay taxes now when you can defer them to sometime in the future? One reason to pay a little more now is if you have room left in a relatively low tax bracket. For example, under current law (in 2019), the lowest two brackets are 10% and 12%. If your taxable income is below the top of the 12% bracket, it may make sense to *increase* your taxable income to the top of that bracket. The lower tax brackets are at historically low rates. Pay the tax now instead of paying it later at (most likely) higher rates.

  How can you increase your taxable income? Some strategies[22] would include: tax-gain harvesting, Roth conversions, contributing to a Roth IRA/401k plan instead of a traditional pre-tax plan, and deferring deductions into the next tax year.

- *Consider a Roth conversion strategy to reduce RMDs in retirement* – As described in Chapter 3, many retirement accounts have Required Minimum Distributions (RMD). These distributions are, as the name implies, required and are typically taxable at ordinary income rates. Many retirees may not need the full RMD amount to cover their expenses, but they must remove these amounts from their retirement accounts. When added to Social Security and possibly pension income, the result may be an unexpectedly high tax bracket. By converting some pre-tax retirement account to their Roth version, RMDs are reduced or

---

[22] These strategies may or may not apply to your tax situation. Always research and/ or speak to a tax professional familiar with your exact situation before making any changes to your tax strategy.

eliminated as most (but not all[23]) Roth-style accounts do not have RMD requirements.

- ***Fully utilize the "tax window" between retirement and starting Social Security*** – Often, retirees will delay collecting Social Security until their full retirement age or later, but retire from full-time work and live off of savings. Typically, this will create a number of years of very low taxable income. As mentioned above, fill the lower brackets with taxable income from Roth conversions or tax-gain harvesting, for example. This "tax window" is typically short, so be prepared in advance to take full advantage of it.

- ***Plan to use the "itemized bunching" strategy described in Chapter 3*** – Utilizing the strategy of itemizing one year and using the standard deduction in the following year can lead to more overall tax deductions.

- ***Consider recognizing long-term capital gains to utilize the significantly higher 15% capital gain tax bracket*** – Under current (2019) law, married filing jointly taxpayers will be taxed at only 15% for long-term capital gains[24] up to a total taxable income of nearly $500,000, which is much higher than historical brackets. It may make tax sense to sell an investment at a gain to pay the tax at this low rate. If you like the investment, you can immediately repurchase it at the higher price, which will increase your cost basis in the security (this is called "tax-gain harvesting"). By the time you would sell the security in retirement, either the capital gains tax rate may be higher or the 15% bracket may be much lower than under current law.

---

[23] Typically, inherited Roth IRAs (unless a spouse inherited it) and Roth 401k plans have RMD requirements. Please check with a tax professional before making any tax-related decisions.

[24] Long-term capital gains typically arise from investments sold within a taxable brokerage account (not an IRA or 401k plan). Other forms of long-term capital gains also exist, such as selling a rental property or personal residence. See a tax professional for more information.

Closing Thoughts

Again, these are just examples of current tax strategies; some may not apply to your situation while other tax moves may offer you benefits. **The point is this: keep your focus on your *lifetime* tax liability, not just this year's tax bill!** Learn the current law or speak to a tax professional to make sure you're making the right long-term tax decision.

Tax laws will certainly change and you may find, in hindsight, that you should have handled something differently. There is, of course, nothing you can do about that situation. Get informed and prayerfully make the best decision you can based on the information available at that time.

The sooner you adequately deal with the risks in your life, the sooner they may be reduced or eliminated. Get started today!

CHAPTER 8

DEVELOP AN ESTATE PLAN

A good person leaves an inheritance for their children's children, but a sinner's wealth is stored up for the righteous.

PROVERBS 13:22

Facing one's mortality is never met with glee and anticipation, but it is a part of life and certainly a component of biblical stewardship. Should you fail to develop at least a basic estate plan, the state in which you live will impose their laws and make decisions about who is to receive your property and who will raise your minor children. The entire process will be made public via the probate system, which is slow moving and often very expensive.

The alternative is to develop a comprehensive estate plan while you are alive and of sound mind. It is our responsibility to make sure that God's resources in our care are handed off to like-minded believers. Equally important is making sure those left behind, a grieving spouse or child, are provided for financially. Proverbs 13:22 states, "A good person leaves an inheritance for their children's children, but a sinner's wealth is stored up for the righteous."[25] Our view should not just be on our own needs, but on the multi-generational needs of our family.

Fortunately, professionals can provide the knowledge and wisdom we need to properly plan our estate. In fact, we're instructed to seek out proper assistance. "Plans fail for lack of counsel, but with many advisers they succeed" (Proverbs 15:22). This team of advisors should include, at a minimum, a licensed attorney in your state. Others to consider adding if needed: a financial planner and an insurance professional. Make sure both spouses are comfortable working with each member of the team. Your spouse may not have the knowledge or interest in managing certain aspects of your financial lives. However, they will have to take control of those areas should their spouse die first. Having the trusted team assembled before the need arises will make the process smoother and easier for the grieving spouse in a time of great need.

As I am not a licensed attorney, I cannot practice law and recommend specific documents or strategies. However, there are a few items that make sense in virtually every situation and should be investigated to determine if they are appropriate for your family.

- **Prepare at least the basic documents used in estate planning**

Some of the basic documents in estate planning are:

- Last Will and Testament – handles the disposition of your property not transferred by other means (for example, an account held jointly with the rights of survivorship automatically transfers ownership to the surviving account holder upon the death of the other owner).
- Durable Power of Attorney – to conduct your financial affairs while you are still alive and, perhaps, incapacitated in some

---

[25] I am not of the opinion that this verse commands us to skip our children when deciding to whom to leave an inheritance. Instead, I believe this verse is telling us to keep a long-term perspective on our family's wealth. Certainly, families in the Bible kept a multigenerational view. Likewise, we should as well as we consider not only our needs and our children's needs, but also the needs of future generations as yet unborn.

manner. The "durable" POA will still be effective should the person giving the POA lose their mental faculties due to injury or illness (such as dementia).

- Health Care Power of Attorney – names a person to make medical decisions for you if you are unable to do so.
- Living Will / Advance Medical Directive – a document specifying what end of life medical procedures you would like performed or not performed.
- Revocable Living Trust (possibly) – a means by which assets may be held to avoid the public probate process and potentially provide for the financial needs of the survivors.

Failure to have, for example, a valid *will* means that the state will use their "intestacy" laws to decide who gets your assets and, if applicable, who will raise your minor children. Further, gifts to charity or non-family members are generally prohibited when you die without a will. I certainly understand this is not a fun process to go through, but being a good steward requires management of financial wealth not only during life, but also at the time of death. As Christians, we need to make sure that the beneficiaries of God's resources that He entrusted to us will continue to be managed in a God-honoring way.

- **Reduce your exposure to the probate process**

Probate is the legal process through which items in the estate of the decedent are distributed, as well as final bills are paid. Probate offers the benefits of being (generally) fair and orderly and it provides certainty as to who owns what property. However, it is also expensive, slow, and open to the public. You may not want your financial information to be made available for all to see, so consider holding financial assets with "will substitute" structure. These assets avoid the probate process.

Basically, a "will substitute" will transfer an asset to a beneficiary without having to incur the cost, time delay and public knowledge that are a part of the probate process. It could be as simple as owning an account as "Joint Tenancy with Right of Survivorship." Assets held in this manner automatically transfer ownership to the other owner, avoiding probate. Another option is to add a "Payable on Death" clause (for accounts at a financial institution) or "Transfer on Death" clause (for accounts holding publicly traded securities, like a brokerage account) to your accounts. These "will substitutes" will change ownership to the beneficiary without having to go through the probate court.

Please talk to a legal professional in your area to discuss your specific options. Probate laws are established by the states, so each one will be different in small, and sometimes large, ways.

- **Keep account beneficiary forms current**

For many types of accounts, such as IRAs and 401ks, a beneficiary form is completed instructing the custodian who is to inherit your accounts upon your death. Often, life events may warrant changes as to who is named on those forms. However, changing the forms is often overlooked.

Take time to periodically review and update your beneficiary forms. It is normally a simple, no-cost process and will make sure that God's resources go where He would have them.

- **Make desired charitable contributions after death from pre-tax retirement accounts instead of from brokerage accounts, Roth-style accounts, or from life insurance proceeds.**

If you plan to leave a portion of your estate to a charity, leave them assets from any pre-tax retirement account, like your traditional IRA or 401k plan from work. As charities are nonprofit, they do not pay income or capital gains taxes. It's better to leave assets that would be taxed at ordinary income rates to a charity than to other heirs subject to those taxes.

Assets in brokerage accounts will receive a "stepped-up" basis, meaning that the heir's basis in the funds or stocks will be the fair market value as of the date of death. It will not be what the decedent paid for the investment. For example, suppose "Joshua" bought 100 shares of Jericho Wall Demolition for $10 per share, or $1,000, in a brokerage account. Two years later, Joshua died and left his brokerage account to Joshua Jr. On the date of his death, the shares were trading for $22 per share and therefore worth $2,200. Joshua had never been taxed on the $1,200 unrealized gain as he had not yet sold the shares. Junior's tax basis in those shares would be the $22 FMV, not at the $10 per share purchase price. Junior could immediately sell the shares for $2,200 and owe no tax! The $1,200 in unrealized gain is not taxed to anyone, thus the reason accounts of this type should be left to people who are taxed (ex. your family) instead of charities that are not taxed.

Assets in Roth accounts retain their tax-free status. Your heirs will have access to these funds tax-free as well, making it preferable to leave Roth accounts to your heirs, not to charities. Life insurance proceeds are generally tax-free as well, so it makes "tax sense" to designate your heirs as the beneficiary, not a charity.

A tax professional and an attorney are valuable team members to help guide you to the most tax-efficient beneficiary for your personal holdings.

- **Consider a charitable gift annuity if you need income for the rest of your life and would like to leave a gift for charity.**

Should you find that you need additional income in retirement and would like to donate to a charity after you die, research and consider a charitable gift annuity. With this type of annuity, an irrevocable gift is provided to an eligible charity. You will receive an immediate tax deduction for a portion of the gift. The charity promises to pay you monthly income until you are deceased. Any remaining funds are given to the charity to use for their charitable purposes.

In most instances, this should only be considered for a portion of your savings in order to keep some liquidity to meet your needs, as well as to provide an inheritance to family members or other charities (besides the one providing the charitable gift annuity). The larger the contribution and the older the donor, the more the monthly payment will be. Some annuities offer the option to pay until both spouses die, but the monthly payments will be less if this option is selected.

A charitable gift annuity is a realistic option to increase guaranteed monthly income in retirement, *but as always, consult with an investment professional familiar with your exact situation.*

- **Understand if you are impacted by gift, estate, or generation-skipping taxes.**

The details of these taxes are beyond the scope of this book and also may be state specific. Again, be sure to consult a tax advisor familiar with the applicable laws in your state. Under current law, these taxes may be imposed at a 40% federal rate (with possible additional state tax). With rates this high, it's prudent to investigate whether you, or your estate, would be subject to any of these three taxes.

Closing Thoughts

There is no "cookie-cutter" advice to offer to every family as each has their own challenges and situations. The Scripture's stewardship guidelines would include the tax-efficient transfer of the wealth you are managing in a way that meets your responsibilities to God and to future generations.

Should God grow your wealth over time, always view it as He does, from a multigenerational perspective. Make your estate planning decisions with your children's children in mind.

CHAPTER 9

THE GOOD AND FAITHFUL SERVANT

Well done, good and faithful servant!

MATTHEW 25:23(A)

When dealing with one's personal finances, it's easy to focus too intently on the wrong things. It's natural for us to wish to succeed in our financial lives. We need to use our God-given abilities to support ourselves, of course, but we should also look for opportunities that God provides to help further His Kingdom here on earth. That may be through an organized charity or church, or it may be by simply seeing a need in your community and being used by God to work a miracle in someone else's life.

Countless lives have been spent chasing wealth, including my own prior to salvation. Somehow, we think that if we could just reach that next financial milestone or goal, we'll be happy and content. Yet that contentment never seems to come. One verse in particular perfectly described the lack of fulfillment I was experiencing, even as my career and wealth were at their highest to that point in my life:

*Whoever loves money never has enough; whoever loves wealth
is never satisfied with their income. This too is meaningless.*

ECCLESIASTES 5:10

For me, this verse captures the futility of trying to find happiness and satisfaction in earthly wealth. It simply can't be done and trying to do so is meaningless. Instead, invest your time, talents and treasure with God as your advisor. Truly, this will be the best investment you will ever make.

The Order of the Steps in the STEWARD Plan

One of the fundamental principles I've learned through my financial coaching ministry is that personal finance is primarily personal. How the **STEWARD** plan should be applied to anyone depends greatly on their individual situation and personality. Stewardship requires that we work on multiple principles simultaneously. For example, understanding God's goals for your financial lives should be a constant focus of both the most and least wealthy among us. Eliminating potential risks in our lives should be a part of stewardship planning whether we are working to pay off debt or are completely debt free.

In general, I believe it makes sense to follow this rough outline of prioritizing financial objectives for most readers (but certainly not all):

1. Commit to following God's guidelines for stewardship.
2. Prayerfully consider God's desires for your financial life and set your financial goals accordingly.
3. These should be done simultaneously:
   a. Determine which risks you can eliminate or reduce and plan accordingly.
   b. Get your estate plan documented and in place. Our time on earth is short and God may call us home with no notice. We're not guaranteed tomorrow so get your plans in place today.

    c. Plan your spending each month, before the month begins. List tithes and offerings as your first expenditure, not the last if money is available.

4. Have a small emergency fund available to handle sudden needs with cash, not debt. There is no blanket rule for the amount as it's a fact-based decision. Generally, something in the $1,000 to $2,500 is sufficient.

5. Prioritize getting rid of non-mortgage debt.

6. Start investing for retirement, at least enough to capture the company match, if any. Work this up to 15% of your income (or possibly more depending on your situation).

7. Set aside money for future college expenses, if applicable.

8. Pay off your home mortgage. Being mortgage-free in retirement has a significant impact on how much you need in investments.

Dayspring Financial Ministry was started to help fellow believers on their journey to true biblical stewardship. I hope that you'll find that the outline of a Christian's stewardship responsibility as described in this book has been helpful as you prayerfully consider how God would have you manage His wealth.

Fortunately, you're not alone in this journey. God will walk alongside you each step of the way. If you believe Dayspring Financial Ministry may be able to help, please don't hesitate to contact us to discuss your situation and needs.

My personal stewardship goal, and one I hold for you as well, is that one day we will hear God say, **"Well done, good and faithful servant!"**

CHAPTER 10

THE *STEWARD* PLAN IN ACTION

I will instruct you and teach you in the way you should go;
I will counsel you with my loving eye on you.

PSALM 32:8

Many of us learn best when we have examples to read and study. Ideas that are theoretical on paper become real when a person's situation is applied to them. Listed below are various questions that we've answered in the past, primarily on my blog (60minutefinance.com). They don't, of course, cover every possible situation and you should not try to apply the advice given in these examples to your specific situation. Instead, consider them to be illustrations of the *STEWARD* plan in action.

The questions and answers are presented in the rough order that they appear in the *STEWARD* acronym. Some questions may cover more than one principle.

Chapter 2 – Set Financial Goals

How do I prioritize financial goals?

Q. I need to prioritize financial goals that compete with each other. I have $28,000 set up for an emergency fund and about $8,000 currently saved for a house down payment. My wife and I have combined $67,000 in debt, which will take us fifteen months to pay off. After paying off our debt, our immediate goal is to be homeowners and have kids after we have a home. I think we should put the minimum down payment for a house (5%) and start to build a college fund. Without debt, I think we can handle a pretty high mortgage. Considering our financial situation, is paying off our debt, buying a house, and then starting to build up a college fund a good order in which to use our finances?

A. Congratulations on having such a nice income at a young age. Also, it's smart to lay out a specific plan for your financial future! All of your goals make sense and are certainly understandable. I would, however, approach the order a little differently. I believe in the theory that focusing attention on one financial issue at a time creates "wins" quicker. These quick wins keep people motivated through a multiyear financial plan.

Here's how I'd recommend that you approach your financial goals:

1. Focus first on paying off the debts. Keep a small portion (up to $2,500) of your emergency fund in a high-yielding online FDIC-insured bank. Apply the rest of it, and the house down payment fund, to your outstanding debts. Within just a few months, you should have all of the debts paid! If you're reluctant to use your current savings to reduce your debt ask yourself the following question: *If your outstanding debts were only around $33,000 and you had only $2,500 in savings, would you borrow another $34,000 just to add it to your savings account?* Most people

wouldn't, but that is basically what you are doing by keeping so much cash in the bank while having outstanding debts.

2. Then increase the small emergency fund up to three to six months of your essential monthly expenses. With your debts eliminated in step 1, you should very quickly meet this goal!

3. Then focus on building a 10% down payment for a home (20% is even better to eliminate PMI). Keep your mortgage payment to 25% of your monthly take home pay while using a fifteen-year, fixed rate mortgage. "House fever" can easily lead to overspending on a home. The more of your income you have tied up in a mortgage, the less you have available to invest and build wealth! With your current debts paid and your emergency funds in place, saving the down payment should be another relatively quick process.

4. Here's why I don't recommend a mortgage payment greater than 25% of your take home pay. The next step is to work your retirement contributions up to 15% of your gross income (not counting the company match). If too much of your monthly cash flow is committed to the mortgage, you have much less available to invest and build wealth.

5. Once you have children, setting up a low-cost 529 account for them would make a lot of sense. I would wait until they are actually born. Also, while it's great to be generous with your child's education, don't sacrifice your retirement wealth building! They can attend lower-cost public colleges and/or work while they are in school. You will have fewer options available when you retire to finance your expenses!

Again, you're doing a great job. Focus on one goal at a time, though, to rack up a lot of financial wins.

Should I buy a $40,000 new car?

Q. I'm in my early thirties and I have never owned a new car. I just graduated as a registered nurse and will be able to earn between $40,000 and $60,000 a year. I'd like to get a new car, but I am debating between getting a car that costs $40,000 and has a high monthly payment, or purchasing a certified used car that is less expensive. Also, I want to buy a home as soon as I have enough money for a down payment. Is it a wise financial decision to buy a new car that costs $40,000 if I want to buy a house in the near future?

A. As a financial coach, I try to create *"guard rails"* for my clients when it comes to large-ticket purchases like automobiles and homes. These **"guard rails"** are important because you don't want to commit too large a percentage of your income to debt payments. For each dollar you spend on a debt payment (even at 0% interest) is a dollar you can't invest for your long-term wealth building. It's fine to purchase a home with a mortgage, for example, but I don't want the payment to be so large that you're prevented from investing for your future.

When it comes to autos, here's the guideline I recommend. The total of your motorized vehicles (like cars, motorcycles, etc.) should not exceed 50% of your annual income, and ideally, it should be paid for in cash. If you decide to get a loan, it should not exceed a twenty-four-month term. So, for your situation, I'd recommend not spending more than $20,000 for an automobile, and pay for it with cash, or if you must, a very short-term loan.

Personally, I'd rather you save enough to purchase a low-value car (but still dependable) with cash. Then, since you don't have a car payment, continue to save each month toward a "new-to-you" car. After a year or so, trade up in car by using the cash you've saved + the first car. Repeat for a cycle or two if necessary. You may find that you like car #2 or #3 and you stop the process with a nice but less expensive car than you'd have if you spend $40,000 now. This plan gets you to the car you'd like—without debt—and without obligating a percentage of your income to debt payments.

Best of luck and go slow. Consider the opportunity cost of what you CAN'T do because you've spent such a large amount of money on a car. If you run a calculation on what the car payments on the $40k auto would grow to over your career, you may well change your mind that you NEED to buy a NEW car.

How can I reduce my taxable income?

Q. How can I reduce my taxable income? I am thirty-eight years old and have two jobs at nonprofit companies. My annual income is $115,000. I am contributing 8% of my biweekly salary into my 401k, which is not matched by my employer, though they typically deposit about $2,500 annually depending on their financial status. Last month, I paid off all my credit card debt and now the only debts I have are $7,800 on a car loan and $50,000 in student loans. I pay about $1,000 monthly for living expenses. How can I reduce my taxable income? What should my financial strategy be?

A: I'm all for legally reducing taxes whenever possible, but for your situation, I'd recommend that your primary strategy be debt elimination. Focusing on, first, eliminating the car loan and then the student loans will free your future income for wealth building. If you're unsure about this being the best path for right now, consider this question: Would you borrow $57,800 and invest the proceeds? Most people would say no. If you fall into that category, then eliminating the debt makes more sense than investing your free cash flow and letting the debt run for its full term. I have yet to meet someone who is debt free that regrets it!

If your focus is on reducing your taxable income, a couple of possibilities are: (1) increase your 401k contributions to $18,500/year, and (2) if eligible, contribute to an HSA account. But again, I'd recommend that you focus on eliminating your debts as soon as possible.

Chapter 5 – Wipe Out Consumer Debt

Do I invest in my 401k or pay off my credit card debt?

Q. I am twenty-five years old and I have $15,000 in credit card debt. I've started budgeting and saving 10% of my paycheck in a savings account. I now have a little over $1,000 in an emergency fund. Currently, I pay more than the minimum monthly payment. At this rate, it will take me two years to pay off all of my debt. Should I stop saving 10% and instead use that amount to pay off my debt sooner? My plan was to use the money I am saving now to invest for the future.

A. Since you already have over $1,000 in an emergency fund, I would recommend paying as much as you can toward your credit card debt. Eliminating debt as quickly as possible is a great way to improve your cash flow and really begin to build wealth. Once you have the credit card balances paid off, I'd recommend increasing your emergency fund to three to six months of your essential expenses.

If you're unsure about whether to pay off the credit card debt versus increasing your savings, reverse the situation and ask yourself what you would do. Suppose you had no credit card debt and only $1,000 in savings. Would you take a cash advance of $15,000 from your credit cards to add to your savings account? Most people would say no. If you would as well, you have your answer about whether you should save more now or pay off the credit cards.

How should I clear up past due debt?

Q. Unpaid debt from years ago has damaged my credit and some has been charged off. Should I be contacting these collection companies to see if there is an outstanding amount and pay the past due debt?

A. I'm sorry that you fell behind with your payments, but congratulations for wanting to deal with the issue. Here's what I recommend:

- Make sure you have $1,000 in emergency savings collected first. No matter how well you plan your expenses, something unexpected seems to pop up periodically and it's good to be financially prepared.

- If the creditors are not calling right now, the debt may have been charged off. I would not contact them at this time. Instead, I'd recommend you begin to accumulate *"debt settlement"* money. Set aside as much as your monthly budget allows. Keep your spending as low as possible to quickly accumulate extra cash.

- List your past due debt in smallest-to-largest balance order. Once you have about 50% of the smallest debt saved in cash (not counting your $1,000 emergency fund), I would contact the first collection company (the one with the lowest balance owed). Offer them 50% of the amount owed to settle the debt IN FULL. They may well take the offer as they are not expecting to collect anything at this point. Most likely, they bought the past due debt for pennies on the dollar from another creditor, so a 50% settlement deal will turn a profit for them.

- If they refuse, say, "Okay, I'll move on to another creditor." They may quickly change their mind! If they don't, continue saving each month until you get to 50% of the second smallest debt. Then try the 50% settlement offer with the second creditor.

- Once you've made your way through the list, go back to the beginning and make the same offer to any that didn't accept it the first time (again, after you've saved up enough cash to immediately send the agreed upon payment). They may be more willing to accept it the second time around.

Over time, settling these accounts will help your credit score and remove the charge-off from your file. Just remember to "wake up" only one creditor at a time! Make a deal with them (if possible) and then move to the next creditor.

If you reach an agreement with a creditor and are going to send payment, here are some things to remember:

- Only send payment after you have received confirmation IN WRITING that the payment will settle the account IN FULL. An emailed confirmation is fine. GET IT IN WRITING BEFORE SENDING PAYMENT.
- Never allow them electronic access to your account. They may clean you out!
- Go to your bank and get a cashier's check and mail it via USPS Priority Mail. This will give you a tracking number to prove they received it. The cashier's check will keep them from knowing your personal checking account number. It will cost a few bucks in postage (and possibly a fee for the cashier's check) but it is well worth it.
- Keep a file with their written confirmation of settlement, a copy of the cashier's check, and a print out of the delivery confirmation FOREVER. They may pop back up years from now saying you owe them more money. If that happens, send them copies of the written confirmation, cashier's check, and delivery confirmation.

Can I borrow from a retirement account?

Q. Can I borrow from a retirement account as a teacher? I am thirty-six years old and I have been teaching for seven years. I am in need of $5,000 to help cover funeral expenses for a family member. Can I borrow from a retirement account?

A. First, I'm sorry for the loss of your family member. Assuming your plan allows loans (most do, but not all), yes, you should be able to take out a loan. Generally, loans are limited to the LESSER of $50,000 or 50% of your vested balance in the plan. An exception to this limit is if 50% of the vested account balance is less than $10,000. Should that be the case, you may borrow up to $10,000. Note, however, that plans are not required to include this exception. Please check with your plan administrator to verify your options.

Please carefully consider whether taking a loan from your plan is absolutely necessary! While the interest you pay is typically credited back to your 401k account, the more significant potential cost is the lost gains from "unplugging" your investments from better performing assets. These losses are then compounded over the next thirty plus years of your working career.

I fully understand that circumstances may leave you with no other option than to take out the 401k loan, but this should *only be a last resort.*

Should I get a personal loan to pay off my credit cards?

Q. I have $17,000 in credit card debt. Is it worth getting a personal loan to pay that off? The interest rate would be less, but there is also a loan origination fee.

A. Mathematically, I can't tell which is better as some necessary information is not available. The question becomes how much interest will you save over the period of time the personal loan will be outstanding versus the origination fee incurred to set up the loan.

From the practical perspective, I'm not a fan of this strategy. As the saying goes, *"You can't refinance your way out of debt."* Instead, I'd focus on creating a strategy to repay the debt as quickly as possible. Here are a few options to consider: (1) sell unused items around your house, (2) get a part-time job or work some overtime, (3) cut back on expenses for a period of time, (4) temporarily cut back on saving in your 401k/403b/ etc., (5) etc. These are just a few examples, but certainly look at your spending for others that may apply to you. Dedicate the savings or extra income to debt reduction.

The point is to create extra cash flow to pay off the debt faster. The sacrifice won't be for a lifetime—only for a season of your life. The sooner you can get to debt-free status, the sooner you can start to invest and build wealth.

Should I save or pay off my student loan?

Q. I am employed and I have budgeted to save a small amount every month. Should I use my savings to pay off my student loan, or accumulate $5,000 in savings, and then invest in the stock market? I would continue to make minimum payments on my student loan. The interest on my student loans is close to 7%.

A. You're asking a great question that many people wonder about themselves. I'd recommend that you accumulate a small emergency fund (around a month or two of expenses) and then work toward paying off the student loans before worrying about investing. Your best wealth building tool is your income. The quicker you can free it of debt payments, the sooner you can begin to build wealth for you! So, pay the loan before you play the market! Further, your interest is rather high so it would be difficult to expect a higher return from your investments. Truthfully, I would make the same recommendation even if the interest rate was 0%.

When you get ready to begin investing for your future, keep your plan simple and low cost. Index funds (or ETFs) are a great tool—low cost, well diversified, and generally tax efficient. Don't try to outsmart the market by picking individual stocks. Most of the "professional" investors can't do it consistently; you and I probably won't either.

Chapter 6 – Accumulate Diversified Wealth Over Time

I want to invest, but I'm nervous. Any advice?

Q. I would like to invest some of my savings but have no idea how to start. Many of my friends lost money in 2008 and I am a nervous investor. What advice can you give me as I consider investing?

A. I can understand someone being a nervous investor! You are certainly not alone.

First, remember that virtually every investor lost money in 2008. It was hard NOT to do so when the market corrected so sharply. This is the perfect example of why it's so important to understand your risk tolerance. Personally, I didn't sell anything in the 2007–2009 market drop (other than to rebalance my investments, of course). I kept buying shares, even as they dropped in value, and was rewarded handsomely when the market recovered starting in March 2009. While the losses were tough to take at the time, I could handle them because my asset allocation matched my risk tolerance. I personally know folks who sold their investments in 2008 and missed the massive run up in value over the last several years. Why did they sell? Because their investments were riskier than their tolerance!

Secondly, you mentioned investing your savings. My guess is that you're using the terms interchangeably, but to be clear to other readers, investments and savings are different. Savings are for short-term liquidity, like an emergency fund (2), and should be held in FDIC-insured accounts. Investments are for long-term growth (and potential income in retirement), and should be managed with the future in mind. Any funds needed within five to ten years should be *saved*, not *invested*!

So, how do I recommend investing for long-term growth? As mentioned above, understand first your risk tolerance then decide how to allocate your investments. Review my investing fundamentals too. They will give you many great points to keep in mind as you begin to invest. I'm available too if you need some personalized financial coaching. Having a plan is a great strategy for a nervous investor to feel better about moving forward.

Even for those of us who have very specific investing strategies, the market volatility we experienced earlier this year can be tough to take. But if you've diversified your investments properly, you can ride out the storms and enjoy long-term investing success!

Is this still a good time to invest?

Q. The stock market has done well over the last several years. Is this still a good time to invest?

A. It's always a good time to invest in the stock market *if your plans and time frame are compatible with investing in stocks*. It should have nothing to do with how the market has performed recently.

Stocks have certainly grown significantly from their March 2009 lows. Since then the *Dow Jones Industrial Average* has grown from below 6,500 to over 25,750 today. Including dividends, the returns for the last ten-year period is over *13% per year*. Pretty impressive.

I can understand your hesitation with investing in stocks when they have put together such a strong performance. Surely, one can easily think, *As soon as I invest, the market will crash*. It can make the decision to invest a difficult one because you are making it more about your *feelings* than your *plans and time frame*.

Any money that will be needed in less than ten years shouldn't be invested in the stock market. Interest rates are pathetic right now, but if you're saving for a need in the short-term—meaning less than ten years—it makes sense to leave those funds in safe accounts. This would include funds set aside for a new car, a down payment on a home, or college expenses for your kids in high school.

Since you would be investing in the market for at least ten years, don't concern yourself with what the market has done recently and whether today is a good time to invest! When you begin spending your investments in retirement twenty, thirty, or forty years from now, the price you paid for the shares in 2019 will be irrelevant. In fact, if you're young and investing regularly in your 401k or IRA, a flat to lower market works in your favor as you'll be buying stocks on sale. Don't fear the near-term results of the stock market. Instead, develop the habit of investing for the long-term.

Should I buy stocks when I'm four years from retirement?

Q. I am sixty-two years old and my retirement account is heavily invested in short-term investments. I plan to retire in four years. Is it an appropriate time to move some of it into stocks and bonds?

A. Congratulations on nearing your retirement. I'm sure it's an exciting time for you!

So, should you own stocks in retirement? The answer to your question depends upon when you expect to need the funds. If you anticipate having a need for the funds within the next ten years, you should not invest them in the equity markets (stocks). You may want to consider a short-term, high-quality bond fund for a little better yield for a portion of the "less than ten-year" money. Stay away from long-term or junk bonds, though, as they are typically more volatile.

Of course, you won't need all of your retirement funds the moment you retire. You may well have a retirement time horizon that lasts for decades, especially if you're married. The funds that you will use to support yourself in your eighties and nineties can (and should) be invested in asset classes, like equities, that should earn a better return than bonds over long periods of time.

For these funds, it makes sense to invest them in a low-cost, well diversified mix of stock and bond index funds. Be sure to keep this portion of your investment portfolio balanced with your risk profile. Rebalance your investments annually.

Please don't take on too much risk trying to chase higher returns. Yes, short-term interest rate investments are paying extremely low rates, but you can't afford to risk losing a portion of these funds as they'll be needed within the next few years. Take the appropriate level of risk with your long-term assets only!

Should I convert my IRA to a Roth IRA to save on RMDs?

Q. I'm sixty-seven years old and retired, but I'm not collecting Social Security until I'm seventy years old. I am collecting a pension and a spousal benefit from my ex-wife that I started at sixty-six, so my income is low during the next few years. I'm staying under the $85,000 limit to keep my Medicare costs from rising. Should I move the money in my traditional IRA accounts into a Roth IRA account to keep my required minimum distributions (RMDs) low?

A. Great question! You've hit on a great tax saving strategy.

Yes, if you have a period of low-income years, it's a great time to consider a Roth conversion strategy to take advantage of your low-income tax rate. If you find you have room in a low tax bracket, it can make a lot of sense to convert enough of your Traditional IRA into a Roth IRA to "fill up" that low tax bracket. Not only will this reduce your RMDs in a few years, but if the funds are left to your heirs, they will be able to withdraw the money tax free!

As you mentioned, keep in mind the potential impact the conversion may have on your Medicare premiums. Also, understand the impact on the taxability of your Social Security income before completing the Roth conversion. There can be a lot of unintended financial consequences of a Roth conversion!

Prior to 2018, you could recharacterize the Roth conversion up to October of the year following the conversion. Basically, this means you could reverse the conversion and treat it as if it had never happened. With the new tax law, you can no longer recharacterize Roth conversions made after 2017. Therefore, you may want to wait until later in the year to determine the amount of the Roth conversion for 2018 and later years. This will give you a much better look at your income!

Should I withdraw from my 401k and contribute it to a Roth IRA?

Q. I will be fifty-nine and a half years old in 2018. Does it make sense to withdraw $10,000 from my 401k and put it in my Roth IRA account? I will remain in the 12% tax bracket if I take a distribution of $10,000 or less.

A. First, let's clarify some of the terms used to make sure your strategy will work.

You wouldn't actually withdraw funds from your 401k if you want to put them in your Roth IRA. If you withdraw the funds and take possession of them, you would be limited to the $7,000 annual contribution limit (based on your age), assuming you qualified for a contribution.

Instead, you are referring to a conversion. With a conversion, funds move from a Traditional IRA/401k directly to a Roth IRA/401k. Note: this conversion is a taxable event. Importantly, there is no limit to the amount you can convert, although clearly, it wouldn't make sense to do such a large number that it forces you into a high marginal tax rate. Again, the conversion amount is taxable in the year of the conversion!

So, with this in mind, the issue becomes your ability to take funds out of your 401k. Are you still working there? If so, does your plan allow "*in-service*" withdrawals? A plan that doesn't allow such withdrawals—and if you're still working there—usually doesn't allow access to the funds in the 401k in order to convert them.

If you do have access to the funds in the 401k (either because you've left employment or the plan allows for "*in-service*" withdrawals), you can move the amount you want to convert to a Traditional IRA and then convert the balance to a Roth IRA. It makes sense to use up the entire 12% tax bracket as you've suggested.

Additional notes: (1) Be sure you have other cash available to pay the taxes. Don't take the funds out of the 401k or Roth IRA! (2) Remember you may owe state taxes. Please check with a tax professional with knowledge of your specific situation. Be aware that a Roth IRA conversion can lead to other unintended tax consequences. Be sure to do your research first! Doing such a conversion every year, if possible, will go a long way to reducing your RMDs when you reach seventy and a half years old.

Should I contribute to a Roth IRA or 401k plan?

Q. I am married and over fifty years old. My spouse and I file joint taxes. Last year, our gross income was $183,000. We both have 401ks. Our 2018 income will be higher than the $199,000 limit. We are looking to both retire when I turn sixty-five years old. Can I contribute to a Roth IRA? I am ten years older than my wife and we are maximizing contributions to my 401k. Should we also be maximizing contributions to hers?

A. Since your 2018 income is over the Roth IRA limit, neither you nor your wife will be able to *contribute* to a Roth IRA for this year. However, you can do a Roth *conversion* or contribute to a Roth 401k if your (or your wife's) employer offers a Roth option. Also, if you have no IRAs, you can also do a *"backdoor Roth contribution."* Of course, with any of these Roth options, you would owe more tax this year, but have a tax-free savings vehicle that will eliminate the taxation of any future gains (if you follow the Roth distribution rules, of course).

With your level of income, I'd recommend you maxing out your 401k ($24,500 in 2018 as you're fifty plus years old) and your wife's 401k ($18,500 as she is under fifty). If you're eligible for an HSA contribution, do that as well! It is the only "triple tax-saving" option.

Congratulations on your great situation. You have a great opportunity to save a significant amount of money by the time you're sixty-five years old!

Which type of IRA is right for me?

Q. I am planning to contribute to an IRA this year. Should I open a regular IRA or a Roth IRA? How do I decide which type of IRA is right for me?

A. Congratulations on committing to save and invest toward your future. It won't get done without you! But you've hit on an issue for many Americans: our confusing tax system.

Let's begin with describing your options. An Individual Retirement Account (IRA) is a great tool to use for retirement investing. As you mentioned, there are two types of IRAs: the regular (or Traditional) IRA and the Roth IRA. They are similar in that you must have earned income to contribute and they have identical contribution limits (currently up to $6,000 per year plus an additional $1,000 if you are fifty or older). Also, a nonworking spouse can contribute to their IRA as long as their working spouse has enough earned income to cover both contributions. *Each also have some limitations for contributions based on income and the availability of a retirement plan at work, so be sure to research your specific situation before contributing.*

There are two major differences between the two. First, for a Traditional IRA, most taxpayers can deduct their contributions which will lower their tax liability for the year. However, distributions from the Traditional IRA during retirement will be taxable income. For a Roth IRA, you do not get a deduction for your contribution (and thus you will owe more tax on your current year's tax return), but the distributions you take during retirement will be tax free! In essence you can either lower your taxes now but pay more later (Traditional IRA) or pay more tax now but lower your tax bill during retirement (Roth IRA).

The second major difference between the two is the Required Minimum Distribution (RMD) rules. For a Traditional IRA, you must begin to take distributions when you turn seventy and a half years old, even if you don't need the distribution to cover your expenses. As mentioned above, this distribution will be taxable which could impact the amount of taxes you'll pay on Social Security, as well as the premiums you will pay for Medicare among other potential tax consequences. On the other hand, a Roth IRA has no RMD requirements, so you can leave the money to grow as long as you'd like.

Deciding which type of IRA to use

Now back to your question: How do you choose between the two options? A primary factor to consider is your current tax rate. If you are in a lower tax bracket (12% or less), the Roth IRA is preferable as your current year tax savings would be minimal. However, if you are in one of the higher brackets (24% or higher), the Traditional IRA makes more sense due to the immediate tax savings and the possibility of a lower tax rate in retirement.

Other considerations may include whether you have a 401k plan available at work (which may prevent you from making a deductible Traditional IRA contribution), how much you already have in Traditional IRA and 401k plans, and when you plan to retire. Unfortunately, no two tax situations are exactly alike, so the decision can be a tricky one. If the current year tax savings are significant, take the deduction now by investing in a Traditional IRA. However, the Roth IRA is a great option for tax-free retirement income for those who would get minimal tax savings this year.

When is a stock gain taxed?

Q. Though it makes sense that a stock gain is reported when sold, I've always been reluctant to invest via stocks because of the paperwork and anxiety of doing a 1040 reporting each year, whether sold or not. It seems like one can only make "income" when actually sold. But even then, one must have records of both the purchase and sale price and then add in splits, new shares, trades, and dividends. Is anything different with ETF or mutual funds? Does the IRS and investor receive an annual 1099? If one does not itemize, do commissions and fees figure into the taxable amount? Are they automatically deducted from the sale price or do they need to be reported in the year they occur?

A. Thanks for your questions. You need not worry that the record keeping will be too onerous to manage.

First, some activity will have to be recorded on your annual tax return, even if you don't sell the holding. Interest and dividend payments, as well as distributions from mutual funds or ETFs, are recognized as income if the payments/distributions are from a holding in a taxable brokerage account. Such activity for qualified accounts, such as IRAs, does not need to be included on your tax return unless money entered or exited the actual IRA.

If you do sell a holding in your taxable brokerage account, you will need to claim the gain or loss when you file your tax returns on Schedule D. The brokerage company will keep the records of your purchases and sales and will report the activity to you and the IRS via the appropriate 1099. Of course, it's wise to keep your own records to verify if the 1099 information is correct. It's not unheard of for errors to exist on 1099s!

The purchasing/selling commissions are typically figured into the numbers reported, so they are reflected on the 1099 forms. No need to itemize to get the benefit of trading commissions. Investment advisor fees are no longer deductible as an itemized deduction (as of 2018).

Don't fear the paperwork with investing! But definitely prepare yourself for investing, understand what you're investing in, and then stay the course (until a life situation changes). Don't try to time the market. Find the right investment mix and rebalance periodically. It doesn't need to be more complicated than that!

Is investing in dividend stocks a good idea?

Q. I recently heard about buying into stocks that pay out per quarter, or monthly, based on the number of shares you own. I've also heard that these payouts, or dividends, can help in the long run even when it's a small investment. I'm twenty-five and thinking about saving for retirement. Is investing in dividend stocks a good strategy for saving for retirement?

A. Congratulations on starting to invest at such a young age! Stick with it and you'll be in great shape later in life.

Instead of a focus on dividend stocks, I prefer (and recommend) to focus on a "total return" approach. Many great companies don't pay a dividend, or they may pay only a very small one (as a percentage of their stock price). In some respects, growth is better than a dividend if you're investing in a brokerage account! When a dividend is paid, you must claim it as income that year. If a stock grows by the same amount (but doesn't pay the dividend), it's not taxed until you sell the holding. It does make tax planning a bit easier.

There is no magic about a stock paying a dividend. Remember: a stock's price will drop by the amount of the dividend paid. So, if a $10 stock pays a $1 dividend, your account goes from: $10 in stock / $0 in cash to $9 in stock / $1 in cash. So, what have you gained? Nothing of value, other than a tax bill (if you're investing in a taxable brokerage account)!

The hype surrounding "dividend investing" has driven up the price of many dividend stocks. Instead, focus on the entire market by using low-cost total market index funds. You'll still have money invested in dividend paying stocks, but you'll also own a lot of great nondividend paying ones too.

Should I invest for dividends?

Q. I am thirty-five years old and want to retire in thirty-five years. Currently, I contribute 17% of my salary to my 401k with my annual salary being $36,500. I am new to stock investing and wanted to get some clarification on stock dividends. If I bought ten shares of a company at $47 per share, and they have an annualized payout of $1.34, will I receive $13.40 at the end of the year for owning those stocks? Is this basic formula correct or am I missing something? I know there *are costs such as trade fees and capital gains tax and assumption that the stock doesn't tank. But if that is a basic formula, then if I buy 1000 shares of a company at $47 per share ($47,000, assuming I had the money) with a $1.34 annual dividend payout ($1,340 per year), and in five years, that's $6,700. Is this how retirees do it? My plan would theoretically use that dividend payout to buy more shares of the company and keep the cycle going throughout retirement. This sounds too good to be true. What am I missing?*

A. Great question. When a dividend is paid, the share price will drop by the same amount. Example: You own ten shares valued at $10 each, or $100 total value. The company declares a $1 dividend per share. After the dividend, you now own ten shares valued at $90 and $10 in cash = the same $100.

If you've owned the shares for at least one year (so it's a long-term capital gain), you would get the same effect from selling some of the shares. Same example above, but assume the company doesn't pay a dividend. Instead, you sell one share as a long-term capital gain. After the sale, you will own nine shares (still $10 per share since no dividend was declared) worth $90 and $10 in cash from the sale of the share = the same $100. The long-term capital gain and qualified dividend will be taxed at the same rate.

I prefer the capital gain route to the dividend strategy. With the capital gain strategy, stock sales are made (and taxes due) when I decide to act. When you invest for dividends, you receive them (and the tax bill) when the company decides to pay them, regardless of your preference.

Are my mutual fund fees too high?

Q. Every time I make a purchase in my traditional IRA, I'm charged a 5.5% fee by my broker for my investment. Are my mutual fund fees too high?

A. With the vast universe of no-load funds, I would never recommend a loaded fund, such as the one you describe with a 5.5% load. Earlier this year, many investors were frantic when the stock market dropped around 5%. Well, every investment you make in this loaded fund is starting with a decrease in value of 5.5%! Avoiding high fund fees like this is important for the long-term growth of your investments.

Expensive, actively managed funds haven't shown they can consistently beat low-cost index funds! I'd encourage you to reconsider your investment strategy. A well-diversified, low-cost index fund portfolio has outperformed the vast majority of other investment strategies. Of course, past performance doesn't guarantee future returns, but the same argument applies to actively managed funds touting their above average returns in the past! Index investing has grown rapidly over the last few years for a reason—it works!

Should I save in my nonmatching 401k or a Roth IRA?

Q. I opened a Roth IRA years ago. I now work for the State of California and I am enrolled in a nonmatching 401k plan. Are there any benefits in contributing to my employer's nonmatching 401k as opposed to my individual Roth IRA? Is there one that I should focus on first?

A. Generally speaking, if you only have access to a *nonmatching* 401k, I recommend contributing to a Roth IRA instead of the employer's plan. You'll have more investing options at (usually) a lower cost.

A few situations that may make the nonmatching 401k a better option:

1. Creditor protection is better in a 401k plan vs. a Roth IRA. If you have a creditor issue, a 401k may be a better option.
2. Access to a high-paying, stable value fund in the 401k plan. I've seen 401k plans with a grandfathered stable value fund paying 5%! It's hard to pass that up for the cash portion of your portfolio.
3. Access to institutional class shares in the 401k plan. Sometimes the costs of these shares are lower than what you could access on your own, especially if you're just getting started with investing.
4. Obviously, if you're over the income limit for a Roth IRA, go with the 401k instead.

Annuities and RMDs. What should I do?

Q. I have two annuities and a 401k totaling $500,000, a year's emergency fund, and a home worth approximately $350,000. The annuities have a ten-year surrender period. I'm five years into the contracts this December. I will begin RMDs in 2019. I'm currently debt free. However, I plan to do $10,000 in home maintenance projects yearly until they're all done. My pension and Social Security should cover those expenses and I do not anticipate needing the 401k and annuity RMD funds. I also do not plan to start an income stream from the annuities before the surrender period ends. They both have a death benefit and a 10% free withdrawal option that I also don't plan to use. At this point I'm not sure I want to keep the annuities after the surrender period, but don't know if I should start taking the free 10% now and invest it, or wait five years and start taking it then. I want the $500,000 to grow and go to my son and granddaughter. What should I do to make the most of the annuities and 401k money with limited risk?

A. Congratulations on being in such good financial shape! Since you mention an RMD, I assume the annuities are inside of an IRA. I'm not sure why your advisor recommended an annuity in your situation since you already enjoyed tax deferral status via the IRA structure. Further, I assume you mean that you can take up to 10% out of the annuities without a surrender charge.

I'm not sure what your estimated taxable income is currently, but if you're in a reasonably low tax bracket, I'd recommend that you begin to move money out of your pre-tax accounts. This can be done by transferring an amount to a taxable brokerage account (your 401k and annuity RMD can be handled this way). If you have additional room in a lower tax bracket, you may want to convert some of the pre-tax (I assume) 401k to a Roth 401k/IRA. This will move the investments to a tax-free account that your son and/or grandchild can also benefit from after your passing.

Since you are investing with your son and granddaughter in mind, you may want to consider a heavier equity allocation than you would like for yourself. Your life expectancy is probably shorter than your son, and significantly shorter than your granddaughter! Invest with their time frame in mind, not your time frame, if you don't need the money for your expenses.

Investments in a 529 account: How to handle when college nears

Q. My daughter is two years from starting college. I have almost enough to pay for four years of school including my other savings accounts. Should it be all in a money market account? Should any portion be in stock and bond funds?

A. I like your thought process! With such a short time frame, I'd recommend all of the investments in a 529 account be in a money market type account (or other "high" yielding secure account). You can't afford to risk the funds by investing in stocks! Imagine a repeat of the 2008 stock market meltdown just while your child is in college. If the stock market corrected like that just before you needed to pay tuition, you may not have enough available. If you decide to use a bond fund, make sure it holds very short duration, high-quality bonds. But again, I'd recommend staying conservative by using a money market or savings account.

Can my child open a Roth IRA?

Q. My child has a part-time job. Can they open a Roth IRA? Is it a good idea?

A. It's a great idea for your child to open a Roth IRA! The extra years that the money stays invested will help it grow significantly in value by the time they retire.

Keep in mind that all of the regular Roth IRA rules apply, so they will need to have earned income in order to contribute. It can come from a part-time job for which they receive a W-2. It could also come from "self-employment" income like babysitting, dog walking, or cutting grass. Your child will need to claim the income on their tax return in order to be eligible to contribute to a Roth IRA.

You could contribute to their Roth IRA—or match whatever they contribute—up to the greater of their earned income or the annual contribution limit of $5,500 (adjusted periodically). When my kids started their Roth IRAs, my wife and I decided to match their contributions. It helped incentivize them to think about their retirement when they were early teenagers!

Finally, I'd recommend investing the funds within their Roth IRA in a good, low-cost total stock market index fund. Remember: time is on their side and over the long term, history has shown us that stocks have the best returns. Skip the bond funds at their young age.

Chapter 7 – Remove Unnecessary Risk

How much term life insurance should I buy?

Q. I'm going to be purchasing term life insurance soon. How long should the policy be in effect? Term insurance can be as long as thirty years. How do I know which one is correct for me?

A. First, it's a great decision to purchase term insurance instead of expensive policies that combine insurance and investing. I'm a big advocate of keeping the two separate for the vast majority of situations.

Regarding the length of the term for your policy, try to match the insurance policy to the amount of time your income would need to be replaced should you die prematurely. For example, if you have very young children, a policy of twenty to twenty-five years would be appropriate. After that period, your children should be on their own and your debts should be eliminated. Your regular investing over the decades should have grown enough to provide for your spouse or heirs should you die after the policy expires.

On the other hand, suppose your children are already grown and on their own, and you are in your mid-fifties. You plan to retire at sixty-five when your mortgage will be paid off. A term policy of only ten years may be sufficient. By then, your debts would be eliminated and you would have begun retirement (with pensions, Social Security, and investments providing the needed income).

When in doubt, go a little longer on the policy as term life insurance is relatively cheap. It works great as an income replacement tool while it's needed. Hopefully, you are investing regularly, as well as eliminating any outstanding debts and mortgages, so that eventually, you no longer need the policy.

Is whole life insurance a good option for my situation?

Q. I am a single mother of two young children and work as a nurse. Currently, I have a 401k account, a 403b account, universal life insurance through the company I work at, and term life insurance outside of my company. I make about $90,000 a year. Would adding whole life insurance be a good idea for my family and me?

A. What objective are you trying to meet by considering a whole life insurance policy? If you need additional death benefit for your children, buy more term insurance. It's much cheaper. Redirect the dollars saved to more productive areas (ex. investing, building savings, paying off debt [if any]). If your goal is to use a whole life insurance policy as a way to build wealth, I would recommend that you don't do it! The insurance component—which you don't need if you're already adequately insured—is expensive. Generally speaking, the investment options are limited and expensive. As your children age and you build wealth, you may not need to have life insurance in place for your entire life.

Instead, buy enough term insurance to take care of your children should something happen to you before they are independent. Depending on their ages, this may mean a twenty-year fixed premium term policy. For investing, follow a few simple fundamentals: keep expenses and taxes low, diversify and rebalance, use low-cost index fund (like at Vanguard, for example), keep investing in good and bad markets—stay the course, understand your risk profile to determine your asset allocation.

Should you pay off your mortgage with a 401k before retirement?

Q. I'm retiring in October of 2018 at sixty years old. I'll have approximately $210,000 in my 401k. I will be collecting a pension of $3,000 a month, and then Social Security later when I need more income. My mortgage balance is $85,000 on a thirty-year fixed rate loan at 4.3 %. My mortgage payment for my condo is $800. If I didn't have to make that $800 payment every month, my living expenses would be cut in half. (My monthly expenses are currently $1,650). I have $30,000 in savings and no credit card debt. Does it make sense to pay off your mortgage with a 401k?

A. While I am a big fan of being debt free, I wouldn't recommend using a one-time 401k withdrawal to pay off your mortgage. You would need to take significantly more than $85,000 out of your 401k to pay the taxes owed and still be left with $85,000 to pay off the mortgage. For example, if you're in the 33% bracket (combined federal and state income taxes), you must withdraw $127,500 from your 401k to have $85,000 left after taxes!

You may, however, want to consider accelerating the mortgage payoff by using a series of withdrawals over several years. First, I would not recommend taking a distribution for this purpose in 2018. You will have worked ten months this year and will, I'd assume, have a higher tax rate than you would in 2019 and beyond.

Starting in 2019, you may want to consider taking a series of annual distributions and applying the net (post-tax) proceeds to your mortgage. These payments, along with your monthly payments, will pay off your mortgage much, much sooner. However, by spreading it out over several years, you should lower your tax liability (vs. trying to do this all in one year, especially 2018).

Should we buy a house for only four or five years?

Q. My husband and I have no debt. I am twenty-five years and he is twenty-seven years old. We currently have about $70,000 saved between our investment account and a money market savings account. I am contributing 10% to a 401k with a 5% match. Our household income is $65,000. My husband is a PhD student and I'm a nurse. The rent we would pay for a similar-sized house is $1,500–$1,750 a month. If we buy a house, it will be under $175,000. We can afford a down payment that's 15%–20% of this amount. Is this a sound financial decision? We do not want to continue living in an apartment, but we would only live in this house for four to five years.

A. Great question and kudos for planning ahead.

I wouldn't recommend buying a house if you only plan to live there for a few years. Real estate is not liquid and the transaction costs are high. Further, the cost of home ownership is much more than just the monthly payment. You need to consider the extra insurance and property taxes you'll pay. Maintenance costs would be your responsibility instead of your landlords. Repair expenses are your responsibility too, and often, they can cost thousands of dollars. Expecting your potential home to appreciate enough to cover these costs, plus return a profit, may be unrealistic in such a short time frame.

Further, when your husband completes his PhD, the best opportunity in his career field may well be located elsewhere. Trying to sell the home quickly is far from advantageous. Being a long-distance landlord usually doesn't work well either.

I love home ownership and would certainly encourage you and your husband to consider it when his schooling is complete and you both have settled into great jobs. Continue to save for a down payment, keep your costs of living low, and consider bumping up your retirement savings to 15%. And enjoy this time without the burden of home ownership opportunities!

There is no need to feel rushed to make such an important decision!

Take your time and buy a house when it makes sense for your life plans and your finances.

Should I buy or rent a home when I'm in retirement?

Q. Should I buy or rent a home when I'm in retirement? I like the idea of not having a rent payment (that will go up over time) by owning a home. But buying a home would take up a lot of my investment portfolio. How do I decide which option is best for me?

A. Deciding whether to rent or purchase a home is both a financial decision and a lifestyle desire. The lifestyle issue is strictly personal. Do you *want* to own a home? How long do you intend to stay in a home? Is the maintenance and upkeep of a home something you look forward to tinkering with or do you view it as a chore? Do you plan to travel extensively in retirement and therefore don't need a large personal residence (or any at all)? Answers to questions like these are the subjective preferences of a potential buyer. They don't necessarily have a blanket "right or wrong" answer from which to create specific guidance applicable to everyone.

The financial decision can, however, be viewed more objectively. Housing costs are like any other costs, especially to one considering FIRE ("Financial Independence Retire Early"). The core principle of financial independence is the accumulation and deployment of resources, typically an investment portfolio, to meet the life needs of the retiree. For many expenses, the only real choice is to invest for cash flow to pay the expense. Food, for example, has to be bought regularly and there is no way to make a one-time purchase to remove the need.

Housing, however, is different. One may choose to rent, thus creating a monthly outflow that will need to be covered by other assets until death. Conversely, a retiree (whether at an early or traditional age) may elect to dedicate a portion of their wealth to the purchasing of a house. This purchase will lower the potential income from an investment portfolio, but it will also reduce their monthly housing cost outflow, thus requiring less portfolio income. How does one choose?

In my opinion, it's a math question. Compare these two numbers: (1) the amount of money that would have to be set aside to generate income to pay the rent for the location in which you choose to live. If you're an adoptee of the 4% rule, simply multiply the annual rent times twenty-five to determine the amount of your investments set aside and dedicated to housing costs. And, (2) the amount of money needed to purchase a home in the same location. Of course, owning a home costs more than simply the cost of the house. Taxes, insurance, maintenance, repairs, and large replacements (ex. the roof) also must be accounted for. Use the same formula as for #1 for these costs. Calculate the estimated annual ownership costs and multiply by twenty-five. This amount, plus the purchase price, is the amount of your wealth that will be tied to your housing expense.

Which number is lower? Some areas have high rental rates relative to the cost of property, while other areas of the country offer high property costs but reasonable rents. For example, the Atlanta area may allow landlords to price monthly rent at 1.5% to 2% of the homes' purchase price, making owning a home a better option. In my area of central Virginia, rents may be half of those percentages, making renting more affordable than buying.

My recommendation is to first answer the lifestyle question. Often, this will eliminate either renting or buying, not necessarily for the math, but simply because of personal choice. If your lifestyle preference could include either renting or buying, then consider the second question. In most instances, the math will point you in the right direction.

Should I continue to save or pay off debt on my house?

Q. I am forty-eight years old and have about $850,000 invested in a 401k, IRA, Roth IRA, and a SEP IRA. I also have six rental buildings, four of which are paid off. The remaining mortgage balance on *my house is $380,000. Should I stop contributing to my retirement accounts and start paying extra on my mortgage?*

A. Congratulations on building an impressive asset base at such a young age!

No, I would not recommend stopping your retirement contributions. I recommend to my coaching clients (who are still employed) that they continue to save 15% to 20% of their earnings for retirement, if possible. Dollar-cost-averaging into a well-diversified, low-cost index fund portfolio is a great plan for building wealth over the long-term. This also allows you to take advantage of market volatility (like we've seen recently!).

If you have free cash flow above this amount, yes, certainly look to reduce and ultimately eliminate your mortgage, as well as the mortgages on your rental properties. You haven't indicated when you'd like to retire, but I recommend the elimination of debt, including your home's mortgage, prior to retirement. Doing so reduces your monthly cash flow needs in retirement which may produce more tax planning opportunities before RMDs begin.

Should I have a 10% down payment saved before buying a house?

Q. My wife and I are looking to buy our first home. We are trying to decide if it's better to build up a larger down payment or buy now. We have stable income, we save 17% for retirement, and we have six months of emergency funds. It's unlikely that we will move in the next decade or two. We have saved $9,000 for the down payment and we have $12,000 saved for closing costs. The average selling price where we live is about $300,000. Initially, we had thought about waiting another year or two until we had closer to $30,000 (10% saved for the down payment), but if interest rates are going up, does it make more sense to buy now?

A. Congratulations on having done so well with your finances. Your nice-sized emergency fund and healthy savings rate will set you up nicely for the future. You didn't mention it in your question, but if you have any consumer debt, ideally, it should be eliminated before buying a house.

You've brought up a great question regarding purchasing a home. I'm an advocate of having at least a 10% down payment; 20% is better as it avoids PMI, but 10% is sufficient. If you're concerned about how long it would take to raise the 10% home down payment, you may want to consider a TEMPORARY reduction in your retirement plan contributions. Of course, keep contributing to capture the employer match, if any. Again, this would be very temporary.

Other things to consider with a mortgage: I recommend limiting the total monthly payment to no more than 25% of your monthly take home pay. Also, limit the loan to a fifteen-year term with a fixed interest rate. The point of these limitations is to prevent "purchase creep." It's easy to catch "house fever" and then overspend because the monthly payment moves very little for each additional feature and related price increase. Be sure to set your purchase and mortgage limit in advance and then stick to it when house shopping.

How should I invest down payment money?

Q: I would like to invest $264,000 for a year or two until I find a house to buy. I would like to earn four to five percent a year and I'm willing to take a little bit of risk. I'm thinking of a mix of money market and ETF funds. What is the best way to invest this money for this purpose?

A: Thanks for your question. Since your time is relatively short (from an investing perspective), you shouldn't take much risk with these funds. I never recommend equities for investments with a time frame less than five years. Experiencing a market correction just as you need the funds may disrupt your plans for purchasing a home.

Earning four to five percent per year for a couple of years, with minimal risk, is tough in today's investing environment. Online money market funds are paying about 2.5%. CDs are a bit higher if you shop around and are patient. Short-term, high-quality bond funds would carry less risk than a total bond market index fund, but would also carry lower expected returns over the long run.

You may need to adjust your return expectations or show flexibility on when you need the funds. If you are willing to delay the purchase of a home if the market is down, you may be able to add a small percentage of a well-diversified equity fund. But again, it would only be if you're willing to put off buying a home for a few additional years should the market need to recover from a correction. It may be best to ignore the temptation to invest down payment funds if you're sure you want to buy in two years.

Where can I invest home down payment money?

Q. My goal is to save $30,000 to $50,000 for a down payment. I'd like to earn some type of return on the savings because it will be sitting somewhere for a year or two. I will be adding $400–$600 every week. My savings account is safe, but low interest. Is a CD account similar to a savings account, but with an interest rate around 1%? I am open to some risk since my living arrangement is comfortable. What is the best account to keep the money in: a mutual fund, a CD, a savings account, or somewhere else?

A. Great question and congratulations on planning ahead for your home purchase!

Since your timing is only a year or two, in my opinion, stock investing is not a good option. Stock markets can swing suddenly (take a look at the last few days to see proof!). Over time, stocks perform well, of course, but that means ten plus years, not one or two.

Bond funds, too, may suffer in the short run should interest rates tick higher. I'm not trying to *"time the market"* and make predictions about future bond returns! Like stock funds, I'm simply acknowledging the risks that come with using bond funds to hold short-term money.

My recommendation for your home down payment fund would be to use an online, FDIC-insured bank. I love local businesses, but I haven't found a local bank or credit union that can compete with online banks. Just make sure they are FDIC-insured. Currently, they're paying around 1.5%, which is historically terrible but better than CD rates at many institutions—and your money isn't tied up! It's also easier to add to an online bank savings or money market account, which is important as you plan on making weekly deposits. This is a pretty boring option, but sometimes boring is a good thing.

One final word of caution: make sure you create and stick to a budget when you are looking for a house. House fever spreads quickly! Make sure you have a plan…and stick to it!

How can I improve my credit score?

Q. I want to get a personal loan so that I can consolidate my debt into one monthly payment. However, I haven't been able to get approved for a personal loan. I assume this is because my credit score isn't great. Do you have any suggestions?

A. Sorry to read about your credit crunch. Unfortunately, there are no quick fixes for a low credit score, unless there are errors in your credit files. First, check your credit reports for free at www.annualcreditreport.com. If you find errors, dispute them with each of the credit bureaus showing the erroneous information.

If your credit reports are correct, the only way to raise your credit score is showing good payment history over time. Unfortunately, there are no quick fixes! Credit scores are calculated based on these parameters: payment history (35%), amounts owed (30%), length of credit history (15%), credit mix (10%), and new credit (10%). None of these can be significantly improved overnight!

I'd recommend speaking with your creditors about payment plans you both can live with. Then commit to paying as promised! Eventually, your credit score will improve, possibly allowing you to lower your interest costs with better financing terms.

Of course, you can't consolidate your way to being debt free! Focus instead on keeping your expenses low to funnel more money to debt elimination! Work overtime or take a second job—only for a period of time, not for your lifetime—to generate more debt-paying power!

Can I reimburse an old medical bill with my HSA?

Q. I had medical bills from last year that I could not cover with the funds in my HSA account. Can I withdraw from contributions I made to my HSA account this year to pay my outstanding bills from last year?

A. In order for a medical expense to be eligible for reimbursement from a Health Savings Account (HSA), the expense must have been incurred after the opening of your HSA account. So, for example, suppose you opened an HSA account on 1/1/2017 and funded it with $100. Later in 2017, you incurred an eligible medical expense of $1,000, but you paid it with funds outside of the HSA. In January 2018, you contributed $2,000 to your HSA account, bringing the account balance to $2,100. Then you request an HSA reimbursement for the $1,000 incurred in 2017. This would be allowed!

Instead, assume that your first deposit into the HSA was in January 2018 for $2,000. The 2017 expense for $1,000 could *not* be reimbursed as it was incurred prior to the opening of the HSA.

It's a very common strategy—I do this myself—to save your eligible medical expense receipts for an HSA reimbursement sometime in the future. In the meantime, my HSA is invested in low-cost index funds.

Here's what's great about HSAs: Your contribution to the HSA is tax deductible. The growth within the HSA account (from the index funds) is not taxed as it grows. Then, when you finally reimburse yourself ten, twenty, or thirty years into the future, the withdrawal is 100% tax free (assuming the withdrawal was reimbursement for qualified medical expenses, or for other approved items like Medicare premiums!). That makes HSAs triple tax preferenced and they are the only type of account with all three!

Can I retire at sixty years old? What about health insurance?

Q. Can I retire at sixty years old? I'm fifty-nine and a half years old. I have $300,000 in a traditional IRA and $1.2 million in 401ks and would like to retire. My wife does not work. Also, I have preexisting conditions and will need to secure health care until I reach sixty-five. My wife is two and a half years older than me.

A. Congratulations on building such a nice nest egg through your working career!

With history as our guide, we know that a moderately invested portfolio has a safe withdrawal rate of around 4% (the "4% Rule"). Put simply, a retiree could withdraw 4% from his or her portfolio in the first year of retirement—then increase the withdrawal for inflation each subsequent year—and have the portfolio last at least thirty years. (Of course, past performance doesn't guarantee future results, so it's best to review your portfolio annually.)

With this as a guide, your $1.5 million portfolio should be able to provide withdrawals of $60,000 in year one of retirement, with that amount increased annually for inflation.

You don't mention your annual spending needs, so I don't know if this is sufficient. Also, you don't mention if you (or your wife) have any pension income, or if you (and/or your wife) qualify for Social Security. Obviously, these would increase the funds available to you each year once you meet the age requirements.

Regarding health insurance coverage, you have a few options:

1. The ACA exchange – Policies purchased through the ACA exchanges cannot exclude you due to preexisting conditions (premiums can be higher if you are a smoker). Further, depending on your income, you may qualify for a premium subsidy. Visit healthcare.gov when you near retirement to see which plans are available in your area.
2. Some employers offer retiree health insurance.

3. You may qualify for COBRA coverage from your last employer. Keep in mind that it typically lasts for up to eighteen months and it can be quite expensive. It's certainly worth checking into, though.

4. If you are a Christian, you may want to consider a Christian medical sharing ministry. While they are not technically insurance, they operate in a similar manner under the biblical principle of Christians sharing each other's burdens. My family has been a member of such a ministry for several years and has had great success with it!

5. Some part-time jobs offer health insurance coverage. While it may not be your first choice, it is an option to consider for a few years.

The good news is you will be only five years away from being eligible for Medicare. Your wife will be eligible in only a couple of years.

Chapter 8 – Develop an Estate Plan

Do I pay capital gains on inherited property?

Q. My sisters and I inherited our family home in 1989. They have been living in the home since then. We now want to sell. Will we need to pay capital gains tax on the difference from what the house was worth in 1980 and what we sell it for?

A. You and your sister's initial basis in the inherited property will be the value as of 1989 when the previous owner died. Their purchase price in 1980 is irrelevant.

The gain, if any, would be today's selling price less deductions (like the real estate agent commissions), less your basis in the property (the 1989 value), and less any property improvements completed after it was inherited in 1989.

The issue then becomes the taxation of the gain for each of you. It appears that your sisters lived in the property since 1989, therefore, they may be entitled to home sale tax exemption of up to $250,000 each.

Unfortunately, you would not receive such an exemption as you have not lived in the home for at least two of the last five years. Fortunately, though, you will be taxed at the long-term capital gains tax rate, which can be as low as 0% (for federal returns) if your overall income is low enough. Your state may tax you on the transaction. Please check with a local tax professional.

Making long-term care insurance premium payments from an HSA account

Q. Can I use my HSA account to pay long-term care insurance premiums?

A. Health Savings Accounts (HSA) are one of the most flexible and beneficial accounts to help deal with the ever increasing cost of health care. They offer a tax deduction for contributions. The balance grows tax free, and then distributions from the account are also tax free if used for a wide range of medical expenses. Not everyone can contribute to an HSA as you must have an HSA-qualified, high deductible health insurance plan. Those who are eligible to contribute are wise to do so! The account can grow for years and then be tapped to reimburse yourself for old medical bills years after they were incurred.

In regards to your question, yes, you may be able to use HSA funds to pay for long-term care insurance premiums. As always with tax law, there are a couple of conditions that must be met:

- The long-term care insurance policy must be "qualified." This simply means that the policy must follow certain rules, such as only paying for long-term care, not building a cash value in the policy, and having renewals guaranteed as long as the premiums are paid.

  Fortunately, most policies do, but ask your insurer just to be sure.

- The amount of premium that can be paid by the HSA is limited to certain amounts based on your age. For 2019, the reimbursable amounts from an HSA are—under forty years old: $420;

forty-one to fifty years old: $790; fifty-one to sixty years old: $1,580; sixty-one to seventy years old: $4,220; seventy-one or older: $5,270.

If you are married and both spouses have long-term care insurance, both spouses would be able to reimburse themselves from the HSA. Premiums above these amounts are not eligible for HSA reimbursement.

Be sure to consider the opportunity cost if you use the HSA to pay the long-term care insurance premiums. The funds removed will no longer be invested, so the future potential growth in the HSA will be reduced. For this reason, it may make sense to use non-HSA funds to pay the premiums, especially if you're relatively young and would have many years of potential compounding left.

APPENDIX A

Shown below is a sample Investment Policy Statement (IPS). Feel free to adjust it to fit your needs, but most importantly, prepare and commit to an IPS for your unique financial situation.

John R. and Diane N. Public
Investment Policy Statement
Adopted January 1, 2019

Financial account information

- Where are your financial assets located?
  - o Most investing assets are held at Vanguard.
  - o Emergency funds are held at _____, but can be moved to a higher interest rate, FDIC-insured account if available
- How much is in tax-advantaged accounts (IRA, Roth IRA, 401k, etc.) versus taxable accounts?
  - o Currently approximately _____% is in tax free/deferred accounts and _____% is in a taxable account
- How much will you be contributing to these accounts?
  - o Contributions to the tax free/deferred accounts will be based on the available income.
  - o Contributions would first be directed to Roth's (if eligible), then to the pre-tax investments.

o Any remaining contributions would be directed to the taxable account.

Investment objectives, time horizon, risk tolerance.

- Short-term financial goals and liquidity needs:
  o Maintain $_____ balance in CIT (or similar emergency fund)
  o Should the emergency fund balance drop below this amount, the priority would be to return it to that balance.
  o Minimize taxes
    - Asset classes with high tax costs should be held only in tax free/deferred accounts.
    - Taxable investment accounts should hold those investments that have lower distributions and tax costs.
- Long-term financial goals and retirement:
  o Have enough financial assets to retire at ____ years old if desired.
  o Assets (not including emergency funds or house value) should be sufficient to produce enough income to cover living expenses (adjusted for inflation), taxes and reasonable allocation to sinking funds for major repairs and replacements.
  o Barring a change in our health status, the assets should be expected to last until Diane is ninety-five years old.
  o No specific allotment is allocated for inheritances, but where possible, assets should be managed to maximize the value to heirs.

Asset classes to be used and those to be avoided

- Asset classes that must be included in the overall investment portfolio:
  o Use only low-cost mutual funds—preferably index funds where possible.

- o Do not overlap and include as much diversification as possible.
- o Asset classes to include:
  - US Stocks (total, value, small, small value)
  - International Stocks (growth, value, small, emerging markets)
  - US and International Bonds
  - Real Estate (either REITs or rental property)
- Asset classes to avoid due to excessive risk, high expenses, or large tax liabilities, etc.:
  - o Hedge funds
  - o Actively managed funds with high expenses, taxable turnover, or distributions
  - o Precious metals

Asset allocation targets and rebalancing ranges

- See Exhibit for allocation percentages by age
- Minimum and maximum deviations from these targets that will trigger portfolio rebalancing:
  - o Rebalancing analysis to be conducted quarterly.
  - o Any asset class more than 5% from its specified allocation percentage must be rebalanced.
  - o Asset classes less than 5% from their specified allocation percentage may be rebalanced if desired.

Monitoring and control procedures

- Frequency of monitoring
  - o Investments and their allocations will be reviewed quarterly
- Concrete procedures for future changes to IPS
  - o Financial reasons for changing IPS
    - Significant, long-lasting change in income
    - Long-term market performance

- o Lifestyle reasons for changing IPS
  - Significant health changes
  - Death of spouse
- o Reasons *not* to change IPS
  - Short-term market performance
- No market timing of investments is allowed. Stay invested based on planned allocations.

REFERENCES

Anspach, Dana. 2019. *Why Average Investors Earn Below Average Market Returns.* January 28. Accessed July 17, 2019. https://www.thebalance.com/why-average-investors-earn-below-average-market-returns-2388519.

Brainy Quote. n.d. *Benjamin Franklin Quotes.* Accessed June 5, 2019. https://www.brainyquote.com/quotes/benjamin_franklin_138217?img=2.

Burke, Monica G. 2018. *New Report Shows Planned Parenthood Raked in $1.5 Billion in Taxpayer Funds Over 3 Years.* March 12. Accessed July 17, 2019. https://www.heritage.org/marriage-and-family/commentary/new-report-shows-planned-parenthood-raked-15-billion-taxpayer-funds.

Butrica, Barbara A., Howard M. Iams, Karen M. Smith, and Eric J. Toder. 2009. "The Disappearing Defined Benefit Pension and Its Potential Impact on the Retirement Incomes of Baby Boomers." *Social Security Bulletin* 69. Accessed July 17, 2019. https://www.ssa.gov/policy/docs/ssb/v69n3/v69n3p1.html.

Chen, James. 2018. *Active Management.* May 12. Accessed July 17, 2019. https://www.investopedia.com/terms/a/activemanagement.asp.

—. 2019. *Index Fund.* June 11. Accessed July 17, 2019. Source: www.investopedia.com/terms/i/indexfund.asp.

—. 2019. "Real Estate Investment Trust – REIT." *Investopedia.* April 18. Accessed July 17, 2019. https://www.investopedia.com/terms/r/reit.asp.

Cox, Daniel, and Robert P. Jones. 2011. *Plurality of Americans Believe Capitalism at Odds with Christian Values.* April 20. Accessed July 11, 2019. https://www.prri.org/research/plurality-of-americans-believe-capitalism-at-odds-with-christian-values/.

Dictionary.com. n.d. *Capitalism.* Accessed July 11, 2019. https://www.dictionary.com/browse/capitalism.

Haig, Rachel. 2009. *Did You Do as Well as Your Fund?* August 7. Accessed July 17, 2019. https://www.morningstar.com/articles/303206/did-you-do-as-well-as-your-fund.

Hargrave, Marshall. 2019. *Standard Deviation Definition.* May 25. Accessed July 17, 2019. https://www.investopedia.com/terms/s/standarddeviation.asp.

Jacobe, Dennis. 2013. *One in Three Americans Prepare a Detailed Household Budget.* June 3. Accessed July 17, 2019. https://news.gallup.com/poll/162872/one-three-americans-prepare-detailed-household-budget.aspx.

Journal of Marketing Research. 2015. "Paying Off Small Debts First May Get You in the Black Quicker." *60 Minute Finance.* August 12. Accessed July 17, 2019. http://60minutefinance.com/wp-content/uploads/2015/11/new-study.pdf.

Kagan, Julia. 2018. *Defining a Coinsurance Formula.* March 1. Accessed July 17, 2019. https://www.investopedia.com/terms/c/coinsurance-formula.asp.

Lipper Alpha Insight. 2013. "2013 Lipper's Quick Guide to OE Fund Expenses." *Lipper Alpha.* Accessed July 17, 2019. https://lipperalpha.refinitiv.com/2013/06/lippers-quick-guide-to-fund-expenses/.

McWhinney, James. 2019. *Use Dollar-Cost Averaging to Build Wealth Over Time.* March 22. Accessed July 17, 2019. https://www.investopedia.com/investing/dollar-cost-averaging-pays/.

Murphy, Chris B. 2019. *Compound Annual Growth Rate – CAGR.* June 13. Accessed July 17, 2019. https://www.investopedia.com/terms/c/cagr.asp.

NP Source. 2018. *Charitable Giving Statistics.* Accessed July 15, 2019. https://nonprofitssource.com/online-giving-statistics/.

Perry, Mark J. 2018. *More evidence that it's really hard to 'beat the market' over time, 95% of finance professionals can't do it.* October 18. Accessed July 17, 2019. http://www.aei.org/publication/more-evidence-that-its-really-hard-to-beat-the-market-over-time-95-of-finance-professionals-cant-do-it/.

Smith, Tim. 2019. *Value Stock.* June 28. Accessed July 17, 2019. https://www.investopedia.com/terms/v/valuestock.asp.

SSA. n.d. *Disability and Death Probability Tables.* Accessed July 17, 2019. https://www.ssa.gov/oact/NOTES/ran6/index.html.

Tan, Kopin. 2007. *A Bullish Call.* December 17. Accessed July 17, 2019. https://www.barrons.com/articles/SB119768725735731187?tesla=y.

The Giving Institute. 2015. *Giving USA 2015 Press Release.* June 16. Accessed July 15, 2019. https://www.givinginstitute.org/page/GUSA2015Release.

The New York Times. 1989. *Transcript of Reagan's Farewell Address to American People.* January 12. Accessed July 11, 2019. https://www.nytimes.com/1989/01/12/news/transcript-of-reagan-s-farewell-address-to-american-people.html.

Vanguard. n.d. *Investing Truth About Cost.* Accessed July 17, 2019. https://personal.vanguard.com/us/insights/investingtruths/investing-truth-about-cost.

—. 2014. "Vanguard's Principles for Investing Success." *Vanguard.* Accessed July 17, 2019. https://pressroom.vanguard.com/nonindexed/Updated_Principles_for_Investing_Success_4.7.2014.pdf.

CPSIA information can be obtained
at www.ICGtesting.com
Printed in the USA
LVHW081310030722
722672LV00002B/2

9 781400 328079